I0453582

The Descent of the Tzaddik:
A Saint's Tale

by

BARAK A. BASSMAN

TELEMACHUS PRESS

This book is a work of fiction. Names, characters, places and incidents are either the product of the author's imagination or are used fictitiously. Any resemblance to actual persons, living or dead, or to actual events or locales is entirely coincidental.

THE DESCENT OF THE TZADDIK:
A SAINT'S TALE
Copyright © 2025 BARAK A. BASSMAN. All rights reserved, including the right to reproduce this book, or portions thereof, in any form. No part of this text may be reproduced, transmitted, downloaded, decompiled, reverse engineered, or stored in or introduced into any information storage and retrieval system, in any form or by any means, whether electronic or mechanical without the express written permission of the author. The scanning, uploading, and distribution of this book via the Internet or via any other means without the permission of the author and publisher is illegal and punishable by law.

The publisher does not have any control over and does not assume any responsibility for author or third-party websites or their content.

Cover designed by Telemachus Press, LLC

Cover art: Isroel Hopsztajn/Public domain portrait engraving

Publishing services by Telemachus Press, LLC
7652 Sawmill Road
Suite 304
Dublin, Ohio 43016
http://www.telemachuspress.com

ISBN: 978-1-965121-15-3 (eBook)
ISBN: 978-1-965121-16-0 (Paperback)

Library of Congress Control Number: 2025900935

Version 2025.01.17

Table of Contents

The Descent of the Tzaddik:

A Saint' s Tale

I. The Ascent of the Soul

NOACH HAD UNFORTUNATELY received all the good fortune for which he had strived and prayed. After years of diligent study in the *yeshiva* and proving himself to be a fine scholar of the Talmud, the *rosh yeshiva*, the headmaster, had struck an exceptional marriage match for him: Noach would travel to the *shtetl* of P. to become the son-in-law of a wealthy man, the lessee of several distilleries from a Polish nobleman with vast landholdings. His father-in-law agreed to provide him with three years of support to continue his studies in the *bet midrash* in P., after which he would join the family's thriving liquor business.

But his new home left him wearied and melancholy. His wife was only interested in clothes and jewels and vicious gossip—and her mother was no better. His father-in-law cared for nothing but his intrigues in the alcohol trade. Noach would find himself seated between his in-laws, his eyes glazed and his tongue still, as his father-in-law pounded the table about the extortionate practices of the river barge captains who shipped his barrels of vodka and his mother-in-law snickered about how some matron had entered the women's section of the synagogue looking like a bloated, rotting carp.

His heart was heavy as he reflected upon the bitter irony of his fate: As a *yeshiva* student, he had spent his every waking hour studying and debating the words of the *Torah*, and the teachings of the sages of blessed memory. Yet all the while he had dreamed of a marriage match to a rich girl. But now that he had what he wanted, he longed only to be back in the *yeshiva* where the talk was of spiritual matters and not these petty, tiresome complaints and quarrels.

With his soul hungry for sustenance beyond this world of dirt and garlic, Noach took to avoiding his wife and in-laws and instead spending his waking hours studying in the *bet midrash*. Keeping to himself in a quiet back corner, he would pore over difficult and strange books that had been written in wild ecstasy, books that set forth—for those with the fortitude to penetrate their defenses—the esoteric secrets of the *Kabbalah*. And as he read, he yearned to ascend to the higher worlds and lose himself in the ultimate source of all, the Infinite, the *Ein Sof*.

But the handsomely printed books and neatly copied manuscripts on the shelves could only lead him so far. Although he could picture in his mind the glory of the supernal worlds, and his ears could almost hear the singing of the Levites at the gates of the Messiah's Palace in the celestial Eden, there was no teaching he could find that showed him how to free his soul from the prison of his flesh. Instead, the texts all taught the same dreary lesson: Lead a life of humility, piety, and repentance, full of fasting and prayer, and then await your reward in the world to come.

Noach, though, could not bear the thought of the many, many years that stretched ahead of him—years to be spent toiling in his father-in-law's distilleries, attending to a litter of screaming brats, and being nagged by his wife over yet another stupid petty errand. And his time for study and reflection would whittle away to practically nothing—and what good would even that precious little time be, as he would be too exhausted to learn properly.

But then Noach had a stroke of luck. One afternoon, the *shammes* of the *bet midrash* approached him in his solitary back corner bench and softly asked why the young scholar always had such a sorrowful look in his eyes. Noach was unsure what to say at first, but then he suddenly blurted out that his soul was yearning for greater sustenance.

The *shammes* told Noach to follow him to a back room where there was a trap door in the ceiling. After opening the door and climbing up a ladder, the two men entered a dusty attic room lit by a wide and round window. Everywhere around them were piles of manuscripts in Hebrew and Yiddish. This is our *genizah*, the *shammes* explained, where we keep discarded writings in which the name of the Holy One, Blessed be He, was inscribed. As our cemetery is small, the elders of the town chose not to waste any of the precious space there burying these documents and so they have remained here instead. Perhaps there is something among these old papers that can feed your hungry soul.

Over the next several days, Noach carefully sifted through the contents of the attic. Most of the writings had no spiritual value whatsoever—letters between merchants, writs of divorce, judgments in legal disputes over the rights to the profits in tangled business partnerships. But then he came across a letter that a scholar in the town had received from another scholar who was living in the Holy Land of *Eretz Yisrael*, in the city of Safed near the tomb of the mighty sage of blessed memory Shimon bar Yochai. The letter was dated over a hundred years earlier, only a few years after the death of Rabbi Isaac Luria, the holy Ari of blessed memory.

The author of the letter was clearly a learned kabbalist. In Safed, he had come upon certain ancient manuscripts that taught him how to induce an ascent of the soul and travel to the higher realms. To Noach's wonder and delight, the letter then proceeded to set out in meticulous detail exactly how to engage in such an ascent.

Noach carefully folded up the letter and hid it in his sleeve. Later that night, at his in-laws' house, he made a copy for his own use, and then returned the original to the *bet midrash* the next morning. Now his studies focused entirely upon the extraordinary letter. But as he read it over and over again, his despair only grew: For his soul needed both solitude and purity in order to ascend. He would never find the necessary solitude within the *shtetl* of P., as his in-laws' house had a steady stream of noisy visitors, and the *bet midrash* always had gossiping young husbands and old men snoring loudly.

In his gloom, he would take long, pensive walks in the woods just beyond the town. And that was when he discovered the hut in the forest. It was a pitiful ruin—there were holes in the roof, the stove was broken, and it seemed that no one had lived there in many years. But it was a place where he could be alone and concentrate upon the combinations of true and terrible names for the Holy One, Blessed be He, that induce the trance through which the soul may ascend to higher worlds.

Before attempting an ascent of his soul, Noach waited for his wife to begin her menstrual period, so that she would be forbidden to him. Freed from the conjugal duties that would have kept him from achieving the necessary purity, he immersed himself in the waters of the *mikveh* and prayed in the synagogue from dawn to dusk, reflecting upon each and every sin he could recall—no matter how trivial or remote—and begging for forgiveness. At the same time, he also fasted except for a few drops of water a day to keep his body and soul stitched together.

After three days of thus purifying himself, Noach snuck off in the night to the ruined hut in the woods. By the light of the moon, he immersed himself in the cold waters of a nearby stream, before returning, wet and shivering, to the hut. There, he donned a *kittel*, a white linen robe, which warmed him a little. Sitting alone in the dark, with only a few streaks of moonlight peaking in through the holes in the roof, he concentrated upon the particular combinations of names of the Holy One, Blessed be He, that he had copied out from the Safed scholar's letter and committed to memory.

As he furiously swayed back and forth, light-headed from days of fasting, the Hebrew letters upon which he was concentrating in his mind grew larger and larger until they embraced his soul and lifted it aloft. His body went numb and soon felt foreign to him, as if his soul had been marooned in a stranger's house.

And then it happened: His soul left his body, and flew up through the hut's roof toward the firmament above. It then vaulted past the stars into realms beyond Noach's wildest dreams: Vast gardens of blue and violet and pink, and towering marble palaces, all stretched out beneath a luminous purple twilight sky. He beheld a *yeshiva* where tall men with glowing faces and shimmering robes argued the most subtle points of the Torah. There were immense columns of blue and white marble, and thousands or even millions of souls were hurdling up and down them at frightening speeds.

Higher and higher continued the ascent of Noach's soul. He approached a vast throne, surrounded by attendants and servants of the king. These attendants and servants were each taller than the tallest trees and possessed of a beauty so terrible and severe that Noach's soul trembled in fear.

The attendants and servants led his soul before the mighty throne.

Noach kneeled down before the king.

A servant's hand gently guided Noach's soul to gaze upon the king. The king, in turn, leaned forward and lifted his long, thick black veil so that a small corner of his chin was just barely visible.

Noach's soul then burst into flames—consumed like a drop of rain swallowed by the ocean.

II. Awakening

WHEN NOACH AWOKE again, the sun was shining brightly through the holes in the roof of the hut. He did not know how or when his soul had returned to his body. He could recall only a few, fleeting details from his soul's ascent—the beauty of a marble palace, the scent of a fruit tree, the song of a happy soul floating up to Paradise—while the rest of his memories were quickly slipping away from him. As he rubbed the sleep from his eyes, he reflected: It is as if I had been invited by the king to a grand banquet and given many presents—clothes and money and jewels—but the royal guards stripped me of almost all the king's gifts as I departed from the palace gates.

With sharp pains shooting through his stiff lower back, he slowly sat up. He had been lying on the dirt floor—for how long, he had no idea. After he pulled himself upright and stood up again, he changed out of his *kittel* and back into his clothes. He then walked over to the small table in the center of the hut where he had left his copy of the Safed scholar's letter. Noach looked down again at the combinations of holy names and tried concentrating on them in the hope of recovering a clearer memory of the heavenly bliss he had briefly tasted. But he was so exhausted that the Hebrew letters blurred and swam and finally evaporated before his disappointed eyes.

He sighed loudly and started to weep. He had been certain that if only he could ascend and dissolve himself into the *Ein Sof*, the Infinite One and Source of All in His Throne of Glory, he would then finally be freed from his gnawing, painful hunger for spiritual sustenance. But even though he had vaulted his soul up into Paradise, it was now more famished than before—as if he had sampled the most extraordinary dishes at the king's table only to be cast back down into his impoverished village with nothing to eat but moldy black bread. And knowing just how exquisite were the delicacies at the royal banquet made his black bread far more bitter to the taste than it had ever been before.

And what was going to happen now? He would walk back home to his in-laws' house. His wife would rebuke him for having wandered off to who knows where in the middle of the night and come back smelling like a filthy peasant. Even if he tried to tell her about the supernal realms that he had glimpsed during his soul's ascent, she would just say that he had drunk too much whiskey and needed to stop making a fool of himself.

Feeling no desire to rush home and submit himself to these insults—which were already so vivid and clear in his imagination—Noach sat down again on the dirt floor. He sighed and stared ahead at a blank spot on the opposite wall.

However, Noach's reverie abruptly ended when the door to the hut burst open and an old Jewish beggar limped inside. The man was a hideous sight to behold. His skin was covered in open, puss-oozing sores and lesions, and one of his eyeballs was hideously swollen and completely white.

The beggar walked over to Noach and asked him if he had any bread to spare.

Noach looked up and shook his head no.

The stranger grunted and snorted in response, and then proceeded to rummage around the room. When he reached the table in the middle of the hut and spied the neatly copied Hebrew letter, he said: You are out here alone, with no food or drink or firewood. But you have these Hebrew writings. You must be a holy man, a *tzaddik*. Maybe you are a hidden saint? Give me your blessing. I won't leave without your blessing.

But Noach did not feel like blessing anyone. And why should he bless this *schlemiel*? He told the beggar to go away and leave him be.

The beggar, though, would not budge. He demanded, adamantly, indignantly, to receive Noach's blessing. As Noach was finding the sick old man's company to be increasingly unbearable—if for no other reason, then because of the way his flesh stank—he finally uttered a blessing to make him depart: May the Holy One, Blessed be He, in His Infinite Mercy and Love for all His Children Israel, heal your body of its many afflictions and bind you in the bond of eternal life.

The beggar bowed his head, thanked Noach, and limped his way out of the hut.

Relieved to be alone again, and exhausted from his earlier crying and despairing, Noach fell into a dark, dreamless sleep.

III. A Saint is Revealed

NOACH AWOKE AGAIN to the sound of voices shouting in the distance. Seeing that the light spilling into the hut was now the pink of dusk, he decided to rouse himself and return home—he had been away too long. But who, he wondered, were those voices? Who would be out in the middle of the woods, especially with the sun fading? Maybe his wife and in-laws were worried something terrible had happened to him, and these were the search parties they had sent out to find him?

He needed to leave at once, and go back home and apologize for his silly behavior. He was no great kabbalistic master communing with the higher realms. He was just an ordinary Jew, in an ordinary *shtetl* in Poland, who should learn to appreciate his wife and ask his father-in-law to teach him how to manage a distillery. He would be a father and a husband and work in his father-in-law's business—and what was so wrong with that?

But first, he had to leave the hut. With sharp pains once more shooting down his stiff back, Noach slowly pulled himself upright, put the copy of the Hebrew letter back in his pocket, and strode gingerly out the door and into the woods.

Once he was outside, though, he was confronted by a large crowd of Jews staring and pointing at him. He realized these were the voices he had heard.

Noach said to them: I assume you are the search party sent out by my father-in-law? *Nu*, here I am. I am sorry to have troubled everyone. I am safe and sound, as your eyes can see, and I am returning home. I am quite weak, however, and could use something to eat or drink, if any of you might be carrying a crust of bread he could share? Or a little brandy?

But instead of greeting him in return, the people in the crowd exchanged confused looks. Then a man stepped forward from the throng. He bore a striking resemblance to the beggar who had barged into Noach's hut earlier that day, but unlike the beggar he had no limp, there were no sores or lesions on his skin, and his eyeballs both looked normal. This man loudly cleared his throat and said to Noach: Holy *tzaddik*, wondrous saint, light of our Exile and pillar of the generation, I was not sent here by your father-in-law. I don't know your father-in-law. I don't even know your name. When I entered your hut earlier today, I was too ashamed of my wretched appearance to introduce myself properly and ask you for your name. But you, great *tzaddik*, in your mercy and your kindness, gave me your blessing. And that blessing has power—such power! I have walked with a limp ever since I fell off a rooftop as a little boy. I have been afflicted with disease, too, for many years, and my skin was covered with boils and sores. Puss and blood poured forth all over my body. The most vicious dogs ran away from me in terror, and the *shammes* would not permit me to stay with the other beggars in the synagogue because my hideous flesh frightened them so much that they would remain awake all through the night, moaning and screaming.

But now I am healed—completely healed—no limp, no diseases. Never before have I felt such joy in walking about and breathing in the air. And what was the cause of this miracle? Your blessing, holy *tzaddik*. And so, I came back to thank you. On my way, one or two people who knew me saw that my limp had gone and that my skin had become healthy and pink. They asked me what had happened and I told them. And once they heard of this miracle, they must have told others, and those others told some more.

And as a result of all that telling, this crowd gathered in front of your hut. I am sorry for that—I know you are a humble man and don't want so much attention. But maybe they need help, too? Or their children? Perhaps you could spare some more blessings?

A clamor immediately arose from the crowd, as everyone at the same time started to shout out their ailments or their loved ones' sufferings and diseases.

Noach thought this was crazy—for how could his blessing have the power to work miracles? He was no saint. To the contrary, he had spent the entire day despairing of his pitifully meager spiritual worth. Nevertheless, the beggar had been miraculously healed of his ailments. How had that happened? Or maybe the beggar had not been quite as sick as Noach remembered?

He needed to return home and get some food and drink and rest—especially food, for days of fasting had left him so light-headed that he could no longer trust what his eyes saw and his ears heard. So, Noach ignored the beggar and all the others and walked toward the path that led back to his town. But his way was quickly blocked by the mob of Jews screaming at him to bless or heal this person or that person. Noach tried to push them away but they grabbed at him with a terrifying strength born of desperation.

To Noach's relief, the old beggar stepped forward again and told the others to keep their dirty hands off the holy *tzaddik*. Then he turned around and asked Noach if he would maybe agree to let these Jews walk by his side as he returned home? And while they walked, they could tell him of their sufferings and perhaps he could offer some blessings along the way? After all, a *tzaddik* can walk and bless at the same time.

Desperate to be freed from the grip of the swarming mass blocking his way, Noach immediately agreed.

The crowd, with Noach in the middle, slowly lurched forward along the path back to the town. As he went, there were so many voices buzzing in his ear—a beloved child stricken with fever; a husband who had been trampled by a horse and could not leave his bed anymore; a mother who screamed in pain all through the night; and so on and so forth.

Noach reached out and put his hands on whatever shoulders and foreheads were within easy reach and shouted out blessings imploring the Holy One, Blessed be He, to cure these illnesses and heal these wounds and have mercy upon the afflicted. And the person so blessed would cry out in gratitude and run off. In fact, so successful was Noach in ridding himself of these people through his blessings that, by the time he reached the outskirts of the town, he was alone again except for the old beggar.

Noach told the beggar that he wished to proceed the rest of the way by himself. The beggar dropped to his knees and kissed Noach's feet. Thank you, great *tzaddik*, he said. Tonight, I will knock on the door of the *shammes* and I am sure that this time he will permit me to stay in the synagogue with the other poor. I feel so strong that maybe I will even be able to find work—to earn my own livelihood. Perhaps I could be a water carrier and find a lonely widow to wed. We could be a comfort to each other. But I will not trouble you anymore—I am sure you must attend to mighty spiritual matters that are beyond my ignorant soul.

And then the beggar walked away, weeping tears of joy.

The sun had set and the moon shined weakly between the black clouds. Noach was grateful for the darkness, as he could only imagine what a wrinkled, soiled mess he must have looked. He soon reached his father-in-law's house and opened the door, which had been left unlocked.

Almost instantly he bumped into his wife carrying a tray of something or other. She let out a stifled scream, staggered backward, and lay the platter down on a table in the corner. Noach's in-laws and their servants came rushing down, followed by his wife's younger sisters.

They all stared at Noach in stunned silence. Eventually, his mother-in-law softly suggested that his wife Chaya should go upstairs with him to help him change his clothes and clean himself up for dinner.

Chaya took her husband by the hand and led him to their room upstairs. Neither spoke a word to the other until she closed the bedroom door behind them.

Chaya sat down on the side of her bed. She sighed heavily, stared at her finger tips, and shook her head. Even though she was clearly upset, Noach was struck at that moment by how beautiful she appeared—her face was a luminous oval moon, and her figure was tall and slender. Her married woman's wig was off, and her lush black hair fell down in messy waves over her shoulders.

In his mind, Noach sternly rebuked himself: Why had he not been content with his portion in this world? How many sons of Israel merit such a lovely wife—a veritable Queen Esther reborn. And her father was wealthy and would take him into the distillery business, a lucrative trade. These were great blessings. *Nu*, then, why had he chased ridiculous dreams of his soul ascending to higher worlds? And for what? He had briefly glimpsed Paradise, but only to tumble back down again into this lowly material world and feel more distant than ever before from the *Ein Sof*, the Infinite Source of All. Why would his Creator treat him this way? So that he would understand, without a doubt, that he was no great kabbalistic master. He was just an ordinary Jew who should learn to appreciate the blessings he had been given and enjoy them while he could.

Interrupting his thoughts, Chaya now spoke: Noach, what have you done? No one knew where you were. We asked the *shammes* at the *bet midrash*, and the other young husbands who study there—but no one knew. My mother told me not to worry. He is a scholar, she said, what kind of trouble will he get into? He will be back home soon enough. Still, I grew more and more worried. Heaven forbid, could something horrible have happened to you? Could you have been robbed, or beaten, or worse?

And then you suddenly walk back through the door, looking like—*this*. You are filthy. You have been lying in the dirt. Scholar? Some scholar you are. No, I did not marry a scholar. I married a drunken, stupid peasant. I never wanted you. I told my father that another boy at the *yeshiva* was a better match. He was tall and handsome and had dark blue eyes. But no, the *rosh yeshiva*—may his flesh be covered in boils—told my father that you were his most brilliant student and so my father insisted it had to be you. Only the greatest prodigy and genius for his beautiful daughter.

And now look at you. You obviously drank yourself into a muddy ditch with a pack of filthy peasants. Did you grab the *tuches* of the Polish serving girl? Pull her onto your lap like the other drunks, sniff her hair and kiss her neck?

Chaya then stormed out of the room before Noach could answer her. He felt the sting of her sharp rebuke. But he also felt its injustice. Who was she to accuse him of being a drunk and a lecher? She was supposed to be his helpmeet, his support, and she had not even bothered to ask him what had happened. What did she know of the *Kabbalah* and the splendor of the supernal realms and ascents of the soul? It was not as if she had ever studied the holy books. Noach yearned once more to sit in his corner in the *bet midrash*, and imbibe the beautiful teachings of the holy sages of blessed memory—real beauty, spiritual beauty, and not the fraudulent beauty of earthly flesh like Chaya's.

Nevertheless, his belly's growls of hunger drowned out his other thoughts. So, he quickly washed and changed into clean clothes and went back downstairs. As he ate that evening at his in-laws' table, Noach could feel their angry, silent glares boring into his skin. After stuffing his gullet as quickly as he could, Noach said that he was leaving for the *bet midrash* as there was a commentary he wished to consult about a vexing problem in a passage in the *Mishnah*, and he would not be able to get to sleep without seeing the solution.

No one responded to him.

With a heavy sigh, Noach left the house. When he entered the *bet midrash*, the *shammes* was slouched over and drifting in and out of sleep. He also spied a tiny old man swaying over a fat tome. Noach went to his usual corner bench, grabbed a kabbalistic commentary off the shelf, and skimmed the author's florid descriptions of the higher *sefirot*. While his own memories of the ascent of his soul kept slipping away, the descriptions in this commentary were remarkably vivid. Noach wondered: How was this master and teacher of blessed memory able to recall every detail from his soul's ascents? Or maybe he was making it all up and had no idea what he was writing about? But then Noach rebuked himself for slandering the memory of a righteous sage.

He closed the book and put it back on the shelf. Sitting down again on his bench in the fading candlelight, he stared out the window into the dark night. Flooded with despair at being trapped between this lowly debased world and the higher realms of truth which he had grasped so fleetingly and then lost, Noach's eyes filled with tears. And despite his sobs, which he was sure were shamefully loud, no one stirred to comfort him—not the snoring *shammes*, and not the little old man in the opposite corner swaying over his huge book.

IV. Miracles Abound

THE NEXT MORNING, Noach was awakened by his Chaya shaking him roughly and screaming in his ear: Why are they shouting for you? Who are they?

Not at all pleased to be jolted from his slumbers, and, moreover, having no idea what his wife was talking about, he snapped back at her: Why can't you leave me in peace to rest a little?

In reply, Chaya groaned and pointed to the window. Go look for yourself, she said, and then stormed out of the room.

Noach slowly rose from the bed and ambled over to the window. Looking out, he saw a small crowd gathered in front of the porch. He recognized many, although not all, of the faces. Recognized them—but from where?

Then he remembered: From the forest—these were the Jews who would not leave him alone until he had blessed them. What did they want from him now?

After dressing and washing, he walked downstairs to the front of the house, passing, as he went, the livid stares of his in-laws and their servants and his wife's younger siblings—everyone was furious with him yet again. With a heavy heart, he pushed open the door to the porch and silently prayed for the fortitude—or the quick wit— to rid himself of these people once and for all.

But as soon as he stepped outside, the crowd erupted into cheers and blessings and praises for the Holy One, Blessed be He.

Noach yelled at them to quiet down, and they dutifully fell silent. Why are you here? he asked. What more do you want from me?

A man stepped forward—the same old beggar again, the one who had claimed that Noach had miraculously healed him of his sicknesses and deformities. After bowing slightly, he said:

Holy *tzaddik*, great master and saint, the people gathered here wish to honor you, for whomever you have blessed has been cured. Diseases gone, limbs healed, death cheated—if you blessed a Jew, then that Jew was saved. The Holy One, Blessed be He, has not abandoned His people Israel. In His Mercy and Love, He has sent you to us.

And they have told others, many others, about your miracles. More are coming for your blessings. You can heal them, too. You can heal everyone.

Noach looked out across the crowd. Their eyes were filled with adoration and awe—*for him*! But how could his blessing work miracles? They had all gone mad.

Unable to bear any more of this lunacy, he fled back inside the house to the comfort of his own bed, and tried to go back to sleep. Tried, but it was no use. After tossing and turning for what felt like an eternity, his Chaya came back and shook him awake again.

She said: Noach, there are six or seven Jews lying on our porch. They are disgusting—their faces are covered with boils, and their odor is so sickening that they might as well be corpses already. They refuse to leave until they see you. *Nu*, can you get up and do whatever you need to do so they will leave us alone?

And so, Noach once more walked out onto the front porch, where he found the diseased and stinking beggars, just as Chaya had described them. They cried out to him in their misery and implored him for help. With an impatient sigh, Noach turned to each one, touched his forehead, and uttered a blessing.

After he was done, they quietly departed and peace again reigned in the house.

That peace, though, did not last long. By the middle of the afternoon, there was a new group of Jews banging down the door and demanding Noach's blessing. And then it happened again when Noach went to the synagogue to pray his evening prayers.

The next morning was even worse. The crowd had grown larger, and the pleas more desperate. This time, Noach's father-in-law refused to let him leave the house and instead sent for the town's rabbi. When he arrived, the rabbi dispersed the crowd and chastised them for believing in magic rather than putting their trust in the Holy One, Blessed be He. If they truly wished to be cured, he told them, then they should repent and beg forgiveness for their many sins.

The rabbi then entered the house and sat down with Noach and his father-in-law at the kitchen table. Noach felt nervous as these two huge bears of men –with their fat bellies and long grey beards—leaned in towards him. He had always been short and slight, and their menacing girth now made him feel even smaller.

The rabbi said to him: When you came to our town, I was told that you were a fine scholar and an upright Jew. We were proud that a *yeshiva bochur* like you, such a famous prodigy, had made a match with a girl from our *shtetl*. But now, tell me, what have you done? All these beggars swear your blessing has miraculously healed their wounds, cured their illnesses, and rectified their deformities. And they are not shy about spreading their tales of your spiritual powers. So, more will come, the sick, the desperate.

At first, I did not believe these tales. Still, after hearing so many of them, I grew curious. I told the *shammes* to bring me some of the beggars who claimed to have been healed by your words of blessing. And in fact, the *shammes*—who looks after the beggars who pass through our town—showed me where this beggar once had sores, and another had been missing an eye, and a third had formerly been a hunchback. Yet now they were all cured—a miracle.

How can this be? Granted, the Heavenly Court pays special attention to the prayers of scholars. But not this much attention. And you may be clever, but you are no Rambam—you are just a *yingele*. Look at you—skin and bones, and your beard is like cake crumbs spilling from the sides of your lips. How could *you* wield such power?

Then I heard something else from the beggars. They told me that you live in a hut in the forest. Apparently, that was where you performed your first miracle. The beggars were quite surprised to learn that you are actually the son-in-law of a rich man who has given you a warm, big bed in his warm, big house.

I asked myself: What is our delicate young scholar doing in the woods so far from his books and his mother-in-law's fine cooking and all the other luxuries of a rich man's household? *Nu*, Noach? What do you have to say? Why were you in the forest, and how did you acquire these powers to heal?

Noach did not want to answer. He felt that the rabbi—and his father-in-law too—were drilling into him with their eyes and silently accusing him of some unnamed but still awful crime. And could they understand what had drawn him to the woods? His father-in-law was a man of business immersed in the muck of this lowly world, constantly scheming for more money. Nor was the rabbi a kabbalist yearning to cleave his soul to the Holy One, Blessed be He. He was a servant of the rich men who had paid the Polish nobleman for his post and who expected him to watch out for their interests.

The rabbi banged on the table and shouted: Speak!

Noach flinched and then blurted out: Yes, I went to the woods. But not often—I only slept in the hut once—because I needed to seclude myself. I required silence in order to pray with the proper *kavannah*.

At these words, the rabbi and his father-in-law exchanged concerned glances. Then the rabbi said: Tell me everything that happened when you prayed in the forest.

And so, Noach recounted how his soul had taken flight from his body and ascended to higher worlds. But the next day he was harassed by beggars and forced to bless them all so they would leave him alone.

Once more, the rabbi banged his hand against the table. No, he shouted, that is not it! There is more—I know there is more. What exactly did your soul see when it left your body?

Noach sighed and looked at the floor. He wished at that moment that he was a small brown mouse who could escape into a hole in the wall. But on the other hand, why should he be afraid to tell what had happened? He had committed no sin.

So, Noach spoke again and this time he told the rabbi as many details as he could remember, including how, at the very end, he had visited the Heavenly Court and merited a brief glimpse of *HaShem* on His Throne of Glory.

When he was finished, the rabbi nodded gravely and addressed him in a firm tone: Noach, I fear for your soul. You did not ascend to higher worlds. On the contrary, you *descended* to the swamps of *Gehenna*. You are a wise scholar. Reflect for a moment upon what happened:

You left the sanctity of this holy community, with its synagogue and *bet midrash*, and went to a place where no Jews live, and probably no other people either.

You entered an abandoned ruin in the forest—exactly the kind of place where demons lie in wait to tempt men and steal their souls. There are many tales of travelers becoming lost in that forest on dark winter nights, and then suddenly chancing upon a large house with brightly lit windows. Cold, hungry, and exhausted, the traveler knocks on the door. He is greeted by a beautiful widow who permits him to warm himself by her fire and eat the delicious food she has just cooked. After our traveler thaws his frozen flesh and fills his growling belly, she suggests he stay the night—no point in trying to journey through the woods at night, as you will only become lost again and wander aimlessly in circles if a wolf doesn't kill you first. The next thing he knows he is lying down in a soft bed; she is next to him; he cannot resist the smell of her perfume and the sight of her naked body; he grabs her; they sin; and then the truth is revealed—the house is an illusion, and they are lying together in the mud of a swamp full of toads and snakes and buzzing flies. And the beautiful widow is no woman, for now he sees that she is a serpent and her teeth tear at his neck and shoot venom into his veins until he dies and his soul is dragged down to the burning sulfur pits in *Gehenna.*

But the demons were clever enough to realize that a *yeshiva bochur* like you would not be tempted by a woman's earthly, physical charms. And why would you be tempted by such things? You can stay right here, in your father-in-law's fine home, and embrace your young and beautiful wife. No, the demons tempted you with a vision of the supernal realms—a false vision, which is why you have so much trouble recalling its details, for you merely saw shadows and smoke artfully arranged to trick your eager soul.

And then the demons decided to use you to lure the souls of other Jews into sin. How did they do this? By giving you a portion of their power so your blessing can work magical cures. As you work your so-called miracles, you lead the people astray. You become an idol unto them, a new Golden Calf before whom they will bow and scrape, instead of putting their faith in *HaShem.* And their flattery will puff up your pride and lead you to stray further from the path of righteousness.

Listen to me, Noach. You must repent. Beg the Holy One that these healing powers be taken away from you. Do not give anyone else your blessing no matter how desperately they plead, no matter how gruesome their suffering. Repent, now, and turn away from the evil path you have started to stumble down.

V. A Messenger and a Guide
from the Supernal Realms

NOACH PROMISED THE rabbi that he would pray and reflect upon the matter, and then he returned to his bedroom. The hours drifted away and the sun began to set in the sky. Feeling restless, Noach left for a walk. His in-laws and wife said nothing to him as they watched him leave. Wishing to avoid seeing the rabbi again, he swerved away from the synagogue and decided instead to pray his evening prayers in the *bet midrash*.

He entered and joined the small *minyan* there. None of the other men spoke to him, and they departed as soon as their prayers were over, leaving Noach alone with the *shammes*. The *shammes* lit several candles to aid any scholars who might wish to study that night and then he left, as well.

Noach reached into his pocket and found the copy he had made of the letter from the Safed kabbalist. He reread it in search of some clue as to what was happening to him. But the kabbalist had written nothing about what would happen *after* the soul's descent back into the body.

Noach prayed for guidance. Concentrating upon the combinations of holy names in the kabbalist's letter, his eyes closed tightly and he felt his soul float away from his body. He saw the town spread out below him, as if he were a bird flying over it. All around him were souls and spirits swishing through the air. He cried out to them for help—to show him which way was truth and which way was falsehood.

But then he felt his soul stumble and falter, and it fell at a terrifying speed back into his body. Noach opened his eyes and jumped up. As he stood trembling and trying to get used to his own flesh once more, the door to the *bet midrash* swung open and a man entered. Noach figured him for a traveling merchant, perhaps on his way to a fair in one of the neighboring districts. The stranger was immense, taller by a head than any Jew that Noach had ever seen— so tall, in fact, that he had to bend his neck to keep his head from colliding with the ceiling.

This tall man strode quickly up to Noach and said: Reb Noach, it is an honor to meet you. Please, sit down. Calm yourself. Deep, heavy breaths—yes, just like that. When your soul ascends and returns too quickly, your body becomes unsettled. But give yourself a moment and you will feel fine.

We have met before, but you will not remember me. I have witnessed both of your ascents of the soul—first in the forest and again just now. Your piety has elevated you to a high spiritual state. Yet now that you have reached such an exalted level—a level that is like that reached by the mightiest kabbalists of Safed, may their memories be for a blessing—you are confused. And the Jews around you cannot help. So-called learned men like your town's rabbi and your father-in-law are pitiful slaves to their appetites, greedy for money and fine clothes and heavy wines. What can such men understand of what you have seen? Your soul has ascended to the supernal realms, while their souls remain chained by pride and gluttony to the maggots and worms crawling in the dirt.

You are no doubt asking yourself: Who is this stranger and how does he know my name and the history of my soul's wanderings? I know these things because I am from those higher realms—in the Heavenly Court, I attend upon Our Glorious King on His Throne of Glory, the Infinite, the Merciful, the Holy One, Blessed be He. But I am permitted, at times, to descend to this lowest of worlds to aid Jewish scholars who have shown themselves worthy.

During your first ascent of the soul, you rose quite high, to the very edge of the Throne of Glory, and you merited to behold a glimpse of His Presence. You did not see His Face—for to look upon His Face is death. Still, because you beheld His Presence, you inhaled the divine flux of pure life that emanates from Him—the heavenly light that allows dead matter to live and worlds to be created. It is that light, now trapped within your soul, that gives your blessing the power to heal.

In your last ascent, just now, you cried out for help. Your plea shot up through the air—like a bolt of lightning in reverse—to the Throne of Glory. And the Holy One, Blessed be He, in His Infinite Love and Mercy, directed me to garb my spirit in a garment of lowly flesh and appear to you in this material form.

You may call me Berl—for my true name wields such tremendous power that it should not be uttered.

By the time Berl had finished speaking, Noach was sitting down again on his usual bench. While he found it hard to believe that an angel had taken human form and come down to help him, he had not yet had a chance to tell anyone about his second, abruptly shortened ascent of the soul—and yet this Berl knew of it. Could this be a guide for him dispatched from the supernal worlds? Or perhaps this was just a charlatan trying to profit from Noach's sudden fame as a healer?

Berl spoke again: You are not sure whether to believe me. Here, put your hands in mine. I will wield the power of my secret holy name to vault our souls upwards to the higher realms. And then you may behold me in my true splendor.

Seeing no reason to resist, Noach placed his hands on Berl's palms. Berl grabbed them tightly and then shut his eyes. He rapidly mumbled the same two or three incomprehensible words over and over again. Noach's head soon became so unbearably heavy that he had to lay it down upon the table. His eyes shut of their own accord and finally his body went numb.

With a jolt, he felt his soul soar up from his body and through the roof into the sky. Up to the moon it went, and then past the stars, and higher still until Noach found himself walking through a forested path in an enchanted realm.

It was then that he noticed that someone was holding his hand and guiding him forward. Looking up, he beheld a giant in a shimmering white robe whose face glowed radiantly. The giant resembled Berl, but it was as if Berl had a light shining from inside his body that illuminated everything around him.

At the end of the wooded path, they came to a marble palace. The guards silently opened its gates for them, and Berl and Noach walked inside. They entered a wide room filled with other giants in shimmering white robes. Never before had Noach beheld such handsome men. And they also sang beautifully—songs of praise, for the Holy One, Blessed be He, and His wondrous Torah.

However, just as Noach was about to ask them to teach their melodies to him, he felt the ground dissolve below his feet and he fell, at dizzying speed, down through the marble floor to the stars to the moon to the roof of the *bet midrash* and finally back again into his body.

And then he woke up.

Berl was still sitting across from him, and he said: *Nu*, now do you believe me? I brought you to the palace in the World to Come where I dwell with my brothers, my fellow angels. When we are not attending to our duties at the Heavenly Court, we sing the praises of our Creator.

Noach said he saw and he believed.

Good, Berl continued. I can help you. I understand the divine power that swells inside your breast, but the fools around you do not.

Come stay with me. Leave your father-in-law's table. He is too easily beguiled by the illusions of this base, material world. He thinks that, after a couple of years of study, you will want to join him in his business of hawking liquor to drunken peasants. He cannot understand the gift that the Throne of Glory has bestowed upon you. And his daughter, your wife, is no better. She thinks of nothing but pretty dresses and fine carriages. In the worlds of truth, in the higher realms, we laugh at pitiful souls like your Chaya with their deluded worship of physical things—things which were built from the dust and that will just as swiftly fall back to the dust.

I will show you where we will live together from now on. It is not far. Come, follow me.

Berl then stood up and left the *bet midrash*. Noach followed him, partly out of curiosity and partly out of an inexplicable compulsion that he suddenly felt. Guided by the light of the moon, they walked to the edge of the town, where the main street turned into a rough forest path that led, ultimately, to the manor house of the Polish nobleman who owned those lands.

To Noach's surprise, he saw in front of him an immense house—far bigger than any Jewish householder's residence in that *shtetl*. Noach could not recall ever seeing this house before, although it must have been there for a long time; it could not have been built in a day.

Berl put his hand on Noach's shoulder and said: This will be our home. Let's go inside.

Berl bounded up the steps of the porch and opened the doors. Noach followed nervously, scared that they might be trespassing upon a rich nobleman's house and would be soundly beaten for their impertinence. However, far from being beaten and driven out, the servants in the house—of whom there were several—bowed low and greeted Berl and Noach like a pair of visiting lords.

A neatly dressed maid served them a late-night snack of pickled herring, onions, and black bread, with glasses of whiskey to wash it down. Once he was finished eating, a different servant escorted Noach to a bedroom upstairs. He slid beneath the thick blankets and let his body collapse into a warm sleep.

VI. In the Court of the Tzaddik

WHEN HE AWOKE the next morning, Noach was seized with panic. Why had he followed that Berl into this house like a stupid sheep? How was he going to explain this to Chaya and his in-laws? They were not going to believe him if he said that an angel had descended from the Heavenly Court to give him counsel and guidance. Now that he thought about it, he was not even sure he believed it himself—after all, who was he to merit such a blessing? If an angel were to descend to this lowly world, wouldn't he go to the greatest sages of the generation and not to some lonely young *schlemiel?*

Noach stood up and walked over to the window. He could see the reddish light of the early morning sun rising over the tall church spires. He strained to see where the synagogue was—for he did not want to miss his morning prayers—but it was too far for him to make out. Frustrated that the synagogue was blocked from his view, Noach felt a dam of emotion burst open inside him, and he let out a long, raging scream. Then he collapsed onto the ground and began to weep.

The next thing he knew, a huge, hairy hand landed on his shoulder. Noach looked up and there was Berl. On a sudden whim, he stood up and buried his head in Berl's broad chest. Berl shushed and cooed him like he was Noach's mother, and gently stroked his hair.

Berl said: Noach, why such sorrow? You have merited to receive great blessings from the Throne of Glory. You have been tasked with healing the sick and bringing the light of the Holy One, Blessed be He, to souls writhing in pain and despair.

It took Noach another couple of minutes to pull himself together. And then he said: But the rabbi believes my healing powers are a trick played upon me by the demons of the *sitra achra*, the other side. How do I know you are not a demon? I had never noticed this house standing here before last night—is it an illusion wrought by demons to seduce and deceive me? And my Chaya—she is certain to believe that I spent the night drinking. I must renounce all of this healing and ascending. I must pray and atone and cleanse my soul and restore my wife's faith in my righteousness. I must go, now, to the synagogue to pray my morning prayers.

Berl, however, grabbed his shoulder before he could leave. Noach, he said, what is this nonsense you are babbling? We met inside the *bet midrash*. The *bet midrash* has a *mezuzah* on the doorpost. If I were a demon, I would not have been permitted to enter a building protected by the words of the Torah written in the scroll inside the *mezuzah*. And I bore you aloft on my wings for a vision of Paradise in the World to Come—your soul visited the palace in the Garden of Eden where I dwell with my brother angels.

Noach admitted these things were true.

Berl now smiled warmly and said: Come, let us pray our morning prayers at the synagogue.

When they arrived at the *shul*, the *shammes* had just unlocked the doors and the first worshippers were trickling in. Berl and Noach sat down together on a bench in the center of the sanctuary. The other Jews stared at them and whispered amongst themselves. Noach once more felt ashamed and embarrassed. He was sure they all knew he had not slept in his own bed the night before and they were no doubt gossiping about how the famed *yeshiva bochur*, supposedly a great Talmud prodigy, was wasting his father-in-law's money getting drunk with Gentile peasants and who knew what else.

Berl, though, appeared indifferent to the stares and whispers. More than indifferent—he appeared defiant. Berl *davened* so loudly in his booming voice that Noach was certain he could be heard in every corner of the town. The wealthy householders by the Eastern Wall shot disapproving glances in Berl's direction but he ignored them.

After morning prayers, the Jews in the synagogue swarmed around the bench where Berl and Noach were sitting. Noach felt a terrible dread, as he thought he could see the harsh judgments in their eyes. Berl, on the other hand, stretched out his huge limbs, yawned loudly, and wished them all a good morning. He said that he was a stranger who had arrived the night before. Although he appreciated the interest his new neighbors were taking in his welfare, he could assure them that he had secured excellent lodgings at the edge of town—a fine house leased from the nobleman—and he would gladly invite any of them to his table for *Shabbat* dinner.

The town's rabbi stepped forward and addressed Berl: Tell me, Reb Stranger, what is your name and why have you come here? You say the nobleman let you a house—have you taken one of his leaseholds from a Jew in this district? We will not stand by idly and let you steal another man's livelihood. And why is Noach by your side? Do you know where he slept last night? His wife and mother-in-law, righteous daughters of Israel, were sick with worry.

Berl smiled widely and laughed softly to himself, which only seemed to deepen the lines of rage in the old rabbi's brow. Then he replied: Rabbi, I have not come here to steal any man's livelihood. May the Holy One, Blessed be He, bestow His bounty upon all the Jews of this town—may you all merit to be rich men with many sons who live in good health for one hundred and twenty years. Still, you are right to mention Noach. It is for his sake that I have come here. I have heard extraordinary tales told of his healing powers, and I wish to give him a dwelling place to receive the Jews who will seek his blessing. I can certainly understand that his father-in-law would not want his household turned upside down by large crowds of the sick and the crippled begging for a cure. Thus, I intend to set up a court—a modest court—for Noach to receive his pilgrims. His wife and other relations are free to stay with us, but if they prefer their peace and quiet, then they can remain where they are.

Unfortunately, we must be going now. Jews in need of healing will soon arrive and I need to ensure that they queue up in an orderly line to receive their blessings. Noach, holy *tzaddik*, please rise and follow me out.

And with that, Berl jumped up from his seat, and grabbed Noach by the shoulder and hoisted him up, too. With his wide girth and long strides, Berl easily parted the crowd of Jewish householders. Pulled along in Berl's wake, Noach soon found himself back in the large house at the edge of the town.

Berl led Noach to a spacious room at the rear of the house, where he sat Noach down in a large, upholstered red chair. Here, Berl said, you will receive the Jews who seek your blessing. Remember that the Holy One, Blessed be He, chose you for this task.

Noach's heart, though, was full of despair. He recalled the angry glares of the Jewish householders that morning—men who had once respected and honored him—and wondered if he was following the right path. And so, Noach said, with a heavy sigh: I should return to my Chaya and reconcile with her. I will repent and help my father-in-law in his business and ease his burdens. Work, family, children—isn't that what makes for a good, righteous life? I must go away from here—I don't want this healing task—I want a wife and sons.

Berl threw his hands up in the air and rolled his eyes. You are a mad fool, he declared. You merited to receive the greatest of blessings from the Throne of Glory and this is how you pay back such kindness, such love, from *HaShem*? You want to repent—for what? For curing disease and healing deformity and putting an end to suffering? And you would now, in your selfish, petty, fretting fear, deny those same blessings to so many other Jews in need? Last night, a mother cried herself to sleep listening to her tiny son scream in agony from the fever that is so close to snuffing out his little light. You can save that boy's life and bring joy to his mother's heart—a joy that is so profound that mere words cannot capture it. But no, you would rather help your father-in-law squeeze more money from drunken peasants desperate for another glass of vodka. *And this you call righteousness?*

Grant me three days. Spend three days here, and meet with the pilgrims who have come for your blessing. Hear their tales. And then, at the end of three days, make your decision.

Noach agreed. After all, what difference would three days make—the time would fly past before he knew it.

Wait here, Berl said, and then he left. A few minutes later, a trembling young woman entered. Noach asked her to sit down in a small wooden chair in front of him. She obeyed at once and then, without prompting, poured out the tale of her tiny son's illness and suffering. When she was finished, Noach spoke a blessing for the boy's recovery and wrote out an amulet with the secret, holy name of a kindly angel to place under the child's pillow. With tears of hope and joy falling from her eyes, the woman thanked Noach and left with the parchment gripped tightly in her hand.

Many more came to see Noach that day. He heard tales of fevers, headaches, toothaches, back pains, vomiting, cramps, boils, lesions, goiters, gallstones, blindness, deafness, and missing and crippled limbs. The parade of misery shattered Noach's heart. He had of course known that the world was full of suffering, but to see it so plainly, and so much of it at once, overwhelmed him.

At twilight, Berl returned and said there would be no more pilgrims until the next morning. It was time for evening prayers. But Noach dreaded to return to the synagogue and the angry glares of the Jewish householders. As if reading his thoughts, Berl added: We can pray our evening prayers here, in this room. I have *siddurim*. You and I are two. I will find eight more among the pilgrims outside and then we will have a *minyan*.

And so, for the first time in his life, Noach prayed in his own private *minyan*. At the end of the service, he pronounced a blessing of good health upon each man who had *davened* with him. He then studied a few pages from a work of *Kabbalah* before falling asleep.

The next two days passed the same way—blessing pilgrims, praying with his private *minyan*, and then studying before bed.

After their evening prayers on the third day, Berl asked: *Nu*, Noach, what will it be? Will you remain here or will you return to your father-in-law's table?

Noach replied he could not abandon so many Jews who were suffering—how could he not give them his blessing and ease their torment?

Berl nodded gravely and said: You have performed countless miracles these past three days. Your blessings have cured more illnesses than a thousand doctors from the most famous universities in Germany. But what shall we do about your wife?

Noach replied: Please send her a message to come see me. I will tell her everything that has come to pass. She will listen to me and she will understand. She will live with me here, and we will raise our children in this house. Their cribs will be bathed in the divine light of the Holy One, Blessed be He, and their little feet will feel the warmth of His Love and Mercy.

Berl raised an eyebrow and cast a skeptical glance, but the only words he said were that he would send the message at once.

The next morning Chaya and her parents visited Noach. Receiving them in the same room as the pilgrims, Noach recounted how he had been blessed with the power to heal and had already come to the aid of so many. He invited them to join him—they too could devote their lives to working miracles and raising a family in this holy atmosphere.

However, when he had finished speaking, Noach saw that their expressions were tense and grim. His father-in-law stepped forward and spoke: I married my eldest daughter—the apple of my eye—to you because I was assured by the *rosh yeshiva* under whom you studied that you were an outstanding scholar and an upright Jew. I looked forward to having such a learned man raise my grandsons. And I also looked forward to teaching you my business and passing it on to you in my old age.

After all, isn't that what any father would want? And is it so terrible—marry a beautiful girl, join her father's business, and pass your days in happiness and good fortune? Apparently, for you, these blessings were somehow a terrible burden. For you repaid my generosity by going off into the woods to frolic with demons! Although you say your soul ascended to Paradise, only the most experienced and mighty masters of the *Kabbalah* can achieve such a feat. A young boy like yourself, who cannot even grow a full beard, is no spiritual master. When you thought you were beholding the World to Come and the Throne of Glory, you were clearly being deceived by demons. They have given you some portion of their dark power to seduce other Jews away from the Torah—those are your so-called healing powers. Nothing good can come of this. In time, your cures will spawn new diseases. Our rabbi, in his love for your Jewish soul and his yearning to see you walk in the path of righteousness, explained all of this to you, but you would not listen.

And now, you have taken up with this stranger. Who is he? No one in this *shtetl* had ever heard of him before he showed up one night. He no doubt seeks to profit from your newfound fame as a healer. Or worse—maybe he is a demon or in league with them? Who can know? A man with no past, no family, he could be anything. And yet you trust *him*!

Then there is this house, which, until recently, was so rundown that most people did not even notice it. Yet it is suddenly leased to this Berl, who somehow fixes and cleans the house in no time and hires servants? Something is not right here. I may not know exactly the evil you have fallen into, but I can't let you drag my daughter into the sulfur pits with you.

You can come home with us now and abandon all this nonsense about healing powers and pilgrims. Or you can give Chaya a divorce and return her dowry. As the Torah teaches: I offer you a choice between life and death—choose life.

Noach quietly seethed with rage as he listened to his father-in-law's words. He had been tasked with a sacred mission—to bring healing, to ease suffering. How could anyone see these righteous acts as demonic? But then it occurred to him: Perhaps he was being tested. Perhaps the Holy One, Blessed be He, wanted to be sure that His servant Noach would not be tempted to stray from his appointed task—that he would stand unswervingly as a sentry at the king's door.

And so, he replied to his father-in-law that his healing mission had been decreed by the Heavenly Court and could not be tossed aside. This was Chaya's last chance to join him, as he did not wish to be tethered to a wife who refused to support him in his great task. Her dowry meant nothing to him. The Holy One, Blessed be He, gives and takes away earthly riches as He pleases.

Chaya now spoke up, in a quivering voice: Noach, please grant me a divorce.

Noach asked her if she was sure—for there would be no going back.

Chaya said she was sure and repeated her request.

To his surprise, Noach felt a pang of doubt. He did not want to lose his Chaya. Granted, she had not always been the most loving wife, and she could be cruel. But to be without her, he would be . . . bereft . . . alone. Being with her was a comfort in a way that being with Berl was not.

Still, what could he do? They had demanded that he turn his back on the task that the Throne of Glory Itself had set for him.

How could he do such a thing? Every time he would pass a sick child, he would know that he had chosen not to heal that child. His weakness for an easy life—to please his rich in-laws and pretty wife—would doom that child to unspeakable agony and an early grave.

With a heavy sigh, he agreed to grant Chaya a divorce. The color drained from her face, she stifled a tear (from shame or love, Noach could not tell), and she silently departed, leaning on her mother's arm. His father-in-law lingered just long enough to give him one last look of disgust, and then he departed too.

Afterwards, Noach told Berl how hard it had been to let Chaya go. Berl, however, assured him it had been for the best. Her soul root was not exalted enough to be the wife of a holy *tzaddik*. She was not his *bashert*, his destined bride, and the Heavenly Court was no doubt rectifying the unfortunate mistake of their union. She would be given a new husband more fitting for her true, lowly spiritual station.

And what about me? Noach asked. Am I cursed to be alone and childless?

Berl patted him on the back and said: Trust in the Mercy and Love of the Holy One, Blessed be He. When the time is right, He will have you matched to your true bride. Follow the path, continue your mission, and have faith in your Creator. A man is merely dust born from a putrid drop—you cannot grasp the ways of *HaShem* with your finite mind. Trust and have faith.

VII. Splendor and Riches

NOACH THREW HIMSELF with renewed vigor into his sacred mission. Everyday crowds of Jews poured through his doors and fell at his feet, telling him their tales of woe: of boils and lesions and fevers, of hideous swellings and putrid rots, of bones broken, and of senses failing. Noach listened closely to their sorrows and then, with a thunderous voice, pronounced blessings of health and healing.

As his fame spread, the pilgrims who came were no longer only the sick in search of healing. The first Jews to seek a different blessing from him were women who sought his aid to open their wombs. Noach protested to them: My special prayers are for illnesses and wounds. The Holy One, Blessed be He, has permitted me to heal, but otherwise I am merely a man. I cannot cause children to be born.

But the women pleaded that they had traveled many miles for his blessing. He was a holy *tzaddik*. Surely, his blessing would carry special weight with the Heavenly Court? And what did he care, anyway? If the blessing did nothing, what difference did it make to him?

Still, he hesitated. Would it not be sinful pride to presume that he had the power to open wombs that had been sealed shut by Heavenly Decree?

Then Berl spoke up: Reb Noach, *HaShem* will not be angry with you for trying to help a Jewish wife bear a child. That is a great *mitzvah*, to bear a child. You should not scorn such a humble and righteous request.

Berl's words persuaded him—after all, Berl was from the supernal realms, so he should know the truth of these matters. Thus, Noach blessed the women that their wombs would open and they would have many children.

As soon as these women returned to their homes and lay again with their husbands, they all conceived children for the first time. When their neighbors saw their bellies swell and learned of the saint whose blessing had worked such a miracle, the crowds crushing against Noach's threshold grew even larger.

At night, after he was finished receiving pilgrims, Noach tried to study works of *Kabbalah* and tractates of the Talmud and other holy books. But he barely had the strength left to keep his eyes open. He often read barely a couple of paragraphs before collapsing into a deep slumber—only to be awoken by Berl at dawn the next morning to begin again.

The lack of food also worsened Noach's exhaustion. Between daily prayers, receiving pilgrims, and straining to study a little by fading candlelight, there was scant time left for eating. Although every now and then Berl would give him a glass of tea or a slice of bread smeared with chicken fat, the portions were meager and rushed, and he often went hungry for long stretches of time.

His only respite was *Shabbat*, from Friday night to Saturday night, when the pilgrims left him alone to rest. A couple of times he tried returning to the synagogue to pray on a Friday evening or a Saturday morning. He hoped to speak to some of the householders—not about anything in particular, just the weather and a bit of gossip. What a joy it would have been to have a conversation where no one was begging to be saved from unspeakable agony.

In the synagogue, however, the householders glared at him in disgust and kept their distance. Noach surmised that his former father-in-law had poisoned their hearts against him. So, he eventually stopped going to the synagogue and prayed instead with Berl in that same house that he could not seem to escape.

One *Shabbat* morning, as they prayed together, Noach fell to the ground and burst into tears. He cursed the day he was born and said he could not continue—he could not bear the burden of being so alone and so tired. He had been a fool to divorce his wife and had made an even greater mistake by remaining in the town where her father was such an influential man.

He wanted to leave at once and travel back to his father's home in a distant town. His father was a good man, a righteous Jew, who leased a small inn and tavern. He could help with his father's business and arrange a new marriage match, a far more modest one this time—just so long as the girl was pious and kind. And then he could pass his days quietly, peacefully, with his new bride. They would have many children together. He could teach his sons the Torah. What greater joy could there be in this life?

To all this, Berl replied: I will not argue with you. The Holy One, Blessed be He, will always steer you back to the path on which you were meant to travel, whether you go willingly or not. No, I will not argue with you, but I would like to point out some difficulties that I believe you have overlooked. Your father's home is far away, in Lithuania. With the dowry returned to your former wife, you no longer have any money—no money to hire a wagon or a carriage, and no money for food or lodgings along the way.

Noach sighed and fell silent for several minutes. Then he said: Berl, you are clearly prosperous—you lease this house, you pay these servants. Can you lend me the money I need to travel home?

Berl laughed. *Prosperous?* No, I was given a modest portion of earthly wealth to use when I descended into this material form. But I have largely spent it.

Noach pleaded with Berl for help—for he could not continue to live in this manner.

Berl looked down at the floor and stroked his beard. For several moments, he appeared to be deep in thought. And then he said: The only way you can return to your father's table is to get your hands on more money. However, because of the slanders spread by your former father-in-law, the purses of the rich men in this town are closed to you. You must earn the money yourself.

But how can *you* earn money? You know no trade and you have no business.

It seems to me, though, that you could charge a fee for your blessings and amulets. Of course, you don't need to charge the poor, but not everyone who comes to your door is so poor.

In the meantime, while you are still here, why don't you invite some of these pilgrims to remain with you, at least until you are ready to leave? You can study with them, and form a *minyan* when it is time to pray. Perhaps, when the weather is fine, you and your companions could take walks in the forest. Their company will ease the heaviness of your heart.

Noach, however, did not want to be paid for his blessings. He had made an ascent of the soul to learn of the wonders and secrets of the higher worlds—from the purest of motives—and not to pile up riches. But, on the other hand, he was stuck in this lowly world for the time being and he needed to escape this miserable town and any escape required money. He had no prospects or skills other than doling out blessings, so what else could he do to earn money? And as Berl said, there would be no charge to the poor—only to those who could afford it.

So, Noach agreed to begin charging a fee for his blessings.

Over the next several weeks, the coins poured in, as desperate pilgrims were more than willing to pay for a cure for their ailments. After all, so many of them had already paid far more to arrogant fool doctors who had done nothing to ease their misery. Each day, after evening prayers, Noach would sit with Berl and count their money, trying to calculate when there would be enough saved for his journey home to his parents.

But the amount of money went down as well as up. With Berl's funds having dwindled to nothing, they needed Noach's new earnings to pay the servants' wages, for the lease on the house, and for food and drink. And so, the money in Noach's purse kept rising and falling and then rising again.

Nevertheless, even though he could not yet afford to travel back to his father's home, Noach was no longer quite as wretched as he had formerly been. For one thing, the extra money meant more and better food, and a fuller belly lifted his spirits. He was also less lonely. Just as he had suggested, Berl cajoled certain of the pilgrims to remain with Noach. These men were carefully selected: They had to be learned enough that Noach could discuss a page of Talmud with them, but also sufficiently in awe of Noach's powers and fervent believers in his special mission.

These disciples slept in Berl's house and ate at his table and studied with their master and teacher in the late evenings and on *Shabbat*. When Noach was busy dispensing his blessings, they would wander about the town and among the crowds of pilgrims to spread tales of Noach's miracles. They became so attached to Noach that they sold all their possessions back in their home towns and sent for their wives and children to join them.

Unfortunately, these new companions also cost money: Berl was forced to rent another house for some of them to sleep in—as, with all their wives and children joining them, they were now too many for the first house he had leased—and their food bills piled up too. Before he knew it, not only was there nothing left over for

Noach's journey home, but he and Berl were quickly running out of money, as the amount they were charging for Noach's blessings was not quite enough to keep pace with the increasing demands of his disciples and their families and all the other pilgrims.

So, Noach was forced to limit his time for study even further in order to be able to receive ever greater numbers of pilgrims and thereby collect more money for his blessings. Still, this did not trouble him. Surrounded by adoring disciples, he was no longer sure that he wanted to leave. After all, his parents were certain to be upset at the collapse of his marriage. And who could say what slanders about him may have reached their ears from his former father-in-law?

Then something happened that finally alleviated all of Noach's money troubles: One of his disciples had a brother-in-law who was a wealthy man. This wealthy man faced a difficult business decision. His leasehold rights to a Polish nobleman's distilleries and flour mills were up for renewal and he was not sure how to bid. Bid too high and he would lose money; bid too low and the nobleman could award the lucrative contracts to a different Jewish merchant. The disciple urged his brother-in-law to travel to Noach's court, as he was sure that Noach, a holy *tzaddik* with knowledge of truths that were concealed from ordinary men, could guide him in making the right decision.

And so, the wealthy man visited Noach and sought his counsel. Although Noach knew nothing about business—he had never even haggled over a chicken in the marketplace, much less hammered out contracts with powerful Polish lords—he shut his eyes, prayed, and focused his thoughts upon combinations of powerful secret names of the Holy One, Blessed be He. When he opened his eyes again, he saw a number floating in the air above the head of the wealthy man—a number even lower than the lowest bid that he had been considering. Noach told him to bid this number and he would be sure to renew the leasehold agreement at a much greater profit.

Two months later, Noach received a letter from this same wealthy man, in which he wrote that he had followed the *tzaddik*'s advice, bid the outrageously low number—and gotten the contract renewed at a huge increase in his profits. Enclosed with the letter was a donation in gratitude for Noach's advice—a sum so massive that Noach nearly fainted. And as if to prove the proverb that money begets money, this wealthy merchant must have told other rich men about how the holy *tzaddik* Noach had led him to such good fortune because wealthy Jews from all over Poland and Lithuania were soon storming Berl's threshold for an opportunity to speak with Noach.

Now that it was overflowing with wealth, Noach's court grew sumptuous. Only the best meat and the finest wines were served at his table. Every word he spoke was received with awe and wonder. Even when Noach said things that, upon reflection, he thought were foolish, they were treated as priceless pearls of wisdom.

The opinions of the Jewish householders in the town changed too. Seeing so many wealthy men flocking to Noach and paying through the nose for a scrap of his attention and advice, the householders also started to seek his advice and finagle invitations to his table, especially during *Shabbat*. Even the town's rabbi apologized for his past harsh words, and asked for Noach's forgiveness and blessing. In fact, he even asked Noach to preach a sermon in the synagogue so that everyone could hear his Torah and learn his wisdom—an invitation that Noach gladly accepted.

Noach's former wife and in-laws were now the ones whom the town scorned. The householders spoke of how Chaya must have had little faith in the Holy One, Blessed be He, and His Torah, to have spurned a husband who was such a righteous *tzaddik*. There was even talk that her shrewish behavior had prevented Noach from realizing his full powers. When these rumors reached Noach's ears, he sharply rebuked the townspeople for spreading slander. But inside his heart, where no one else could see, he cracked a bitter, gleeful smile.

Although Noach had gained wealth and renown, and his enemies were repentant and cowed, his heart was heavy with regret. Because of the swirl of visitors and blessings and disciples, he had less and less time to study. By the end of his days, he would be so exhausted that he could barely make out a few words of a holy book before he started to fall asleep. His memory of the sacred texts and the teachings of the sages of blessed memory faded and dimmed. He concealed his growing ignorance by answering questions with long, intricate parables that he implied were full of hidden, mystical meaning. He would say that quoting abstruse commentaries on the Talmud left the Torah's wisdom closed off to everyone but the most learned, whereas he ministered to all Jews, even illiterate beggars who could not recite a single Psalm. But even as he spoke these words and wove his elaborate parables about fairytale kings and castles and nobles and princesses, he felt a secret burning shame that with each passing day he was turning into a contemptible, ignorant boor.

So many times, he swore in his heart he would stop this madness—no more pilgrims and wealthy men and disciples and court—and return to his studies. He would take some of the money he had accumulated—not everything, only just enough—and go to a faraway land where he was not known. There, he would assume a new name and devote the remaining days allotted to him to the study of the Talmud and the Zohar and all the other beautiful, sweet words of the sages of blessed memory. Perhaps he would teach a few lessons to children to eke out a humble livelihood.

And he would marry again, as he had grown lonely without the comfort of a wife. But this time his bride would be humble—a plain-looking orphan girl, maybe even an ugly girl—a girl who had suffered much but had a deep and simple faith in the Holy One, Blessed be He. They would have children and he would teach them too.

But then these moods would pass, and he would be swept up once more in the whirl of fawning visitors hurling piles of coins at his feet. And he would stuff his belly with goose meat and spiced wine, and forget all about his dream of holding hands with his plain, orphan bride.

VIII. The Call of Lilith

THUS DID NOACH pass his days in luxury and delight. Yet he was lonely. Noach often recalled the words of the Torah—*For it is not good for man to be alone.* He needed a wife; he yearned for children. He would sometimes ask Berl to fetch a marriage broker, but Berl always had an excuse to delay: The marriage brokers charged such high fees and, just then, Noach's donations were needed to repair a broken roof or feed a group of pilgrims or pay the school fees for his disciples' children. Or if money was not the issue, then it was timing—some major holiday or celebration was coming up and Noach could not be distracted.

One beautiful Spring day, during the *omer* between *Pesach* and *Shavuot*, Berl escorted a new pilgrim in to see Noach and beseech him for his blessing. She was a young woman, and a Gentile, dressed expensively in fabrics dyed a blue as luminous as the sky. Noach surmised she was a rich noblewoman. Like many fashionable Polish ladies, her outfit was far from modest: The sky-blue dress revealed almost all of her cleavage and was cinched tightly at the waist to flaunt the curves of her body. And if that was not enough, her hair was a mass of thick golden curls falling almost to her navel. When she sighed—which was often—her strong perfume blew right into Noach's nostrils, making him dizzy and light-headed.

She sighed often because her son was ill. The doctors—and as a highborn and wealthy lady, she had hired the best of them—had tried all sorts of powders and potions and bled him with leeches until he passed out. But none of it had helped.

She had also sought the aid of her family's priest, who sang masses and prayed day and night for the boy's recovery. The child had been doused with holy water, touched the relics of a holy saint, and been surrounded with rosaries and crucifixes. But once more, none of it had helped.

Finally, in her desperation, she asked a Jewish woman who leased an inn from her husband whether there was a Jewish healer who could help—and thus she had heard about Noach. Could he help her son? The boy was so good—so kind to everyone, so sweet and gentle. He was too good for this wretched world—God must want that precious soul back by His side in Heaven. But can't she be with him a little longer? Was there a way to save her beautiful child?

As she spoke, Noach forced himself to maintain a steely, pensive gaze. But inside, his blood was on fire and his heart was pounding with a relentless brutality: For he could not stop feasting his eyes upon her ample and firm chest and cascades of luxuriant yellow hair.

Still, he rebuked himself: A Polish noblewoman had prostrated herself before him. She must be desperate—for how else could she bear the shame of begging a Jew for a blessing? Nevertheless, should he offend her, take one too many liberties, she would have him clapped in chains and sent to rot in a dank prison cell—or worse.

Noach carefully weighed his words in reply. He deferred to her rank and addressed her as *Pani*; he spoke of how unworthy he was to receive such a noble lady in his simple home. But clearly her son was a special, saintly soul, and he would do everything in his power to heal him. Noach then recited several blessings for the boy's recovery. The noblewoman listened intently and her eyes pulsated with eagerness and hope, although it was obvious that she could not understand any of the Hebrew words. He also wrote out an amulet with the secret holy names that summon the angels who look after the righteous among the Gentile Nations, and he told her to place it under the child's pillow as soon as possible.

Thanking him profusely, the noblewoman grabbed his hand and kissed his wrist, and then she quickly departed. Noach had not expected to touch her—the Jewish women who sought his help were always careful to avoid even the possibility of an accidental touch. The feel of her soft skin and moist lips sent waves of searingly intense pleasure shooting through his veins.

Noach's amulet and blessings worked: By the next morning, the boy had made a complete and miraculous recovery. In gratitude, his parents made a sizeable donation to Noach's court and also pledged to pay for the renovation of the town's synagogue and *mikveh*. The Jewish householders now feted and fawned over Noach like never before, as, thanks to him, they no longer needed to raise the money themselves for these repairs. They also whispered amongst themselves, quietly and discreetly in dark corners, that this nobleman was now in the Jews' debt and would protect them from any enemy of Israel who might try to fan the flames of persecution.

Nevertheless, Noach came to regret the noble lady's visit. Because of her, his dreams soon became a torment of sick, demented lust. Once his eyes shut and his muscles relaxed, he would picture her again in her immodest dress. Only now she was not sighing and pleading for her little son. No, now she was slithering upon him like a snake, writhing, grinding, driving her lips against his and grabbing and squeezing his quaking flesh.

He would awake trembling and sweating. All too often his thigh would be smeared with a nocturnal emission. Upon feeling the putrid, viscous drops on his leg, he would burst into tears and tumble out of his bed onto the floor. Prostrating himself on the ground, he would beg forgiveness of the Holy One, Blessed be He, for his disgusting thoughts and for any sinful acts he may have unwittingly committed while asleep.

Yet no matter how mightily he struggled, he could not rid himself of these vile dreams. And then the same disgusting visions began to haunt him during the day too—when he tried to pray, when he sat with his disciples telling parables. Although he concealed his shame in front of others, when he was alone, he could not bear how vile and contemptible he had become.

Noach concluded that Lilith, Queen of the Demons, had decided to tempt him. She was no doubt furious that the miracles wrought by Noach's blessings and amulets had brought so many Jews back to the path of Torah and righteousness. When, in a moment of weakness, his *yetzer ha-ra*, his evil inclination, had roused his lust at the sight of the Polish noblewoman, Lilith must have smelled her opportunity. In his sinful state, she had found a way to penetrate into his soul and pummel him with filthy, sick dreams.

But Noach was determined to resist her. After closely studying several kabbalistic works that set forth particularly potent formulae for fighting off demons, he wrote out one amulet to expel Lilith and a second to prevent her return. Placing both beneath his pillow, he prayed to the Holy One, Blessed be He, for peaceful, pious dreams.

Nonetheless, Lilith once more invaded his sleep. In his dream, she gripped him tightly and touched him in abominable, unnatural ways. She rubbed her wrist into his nostrils so he would be forced to inhale her intoxicating perfume, and whispered in his ear the exquisite pleasures that he could taste if only he gave himself over to her.

And this time, she brought other demon women along with her, at least four or five of them. All wearing immodest dresses like their queen, with hair—red and blue and black and white—falling down to their waists, they circled around Noach, giving him disgusting, leering looks. When he cried out in his dream for the demon women to leave him alone, they laughed and mocked his lack of manliness—they called him a frightened little girl.

When Noach awoke the next morning, his leg was once more stained with long tracks of thick, sticky nocturnal emissions. Horrified at the state he was in, he reached under his pillow to check if the amulets were still there. Finding them both exactly where he had left them, Noach was overcome with despair—if his prayers and amulets were of no use, then what else could he do?

Noach slid down from his bed onto the floor. Staring straight ahead at the wall, he groaned in self-pity. Soon the groan became a cry, and the cry became loud, hysterical weeping. He heard a commotion in the hallway outside his bedroom; no doubt his disciples and maybe even some pilgrims could hear him. But he did not care.

After a time, Berl came in and sat down on the floor next to him. Taking Noach's hand into his own, he said softly: Holy *tzaddik*, great saint, why is your heart so heavy? Tell me—a man's burdens only grow heavier when he will not speak of them.

With an effort, Noach calmed himself down. Berl was right: He needed the aid of a friend—and what better friend did he have than Berl? The disciples and pilgrims fussed and fawned over him, but they looked upon him as an idol, and not as a man—as a golden calf that spat out amulets and blessings. Berl was his only true friend, who cared for him and looked out for his welfare.

And so, Noach told him everything—how the Polish noblewoman had aroused his lusts, how Lilith, Queen of the Demons, may her name be blotted out, had used this moment of weakness to burrow into his soul and afflict him, and how his prayers and amulets had been of no use.

Berl nodded gravely as Noach told his tale. When he was finished, Berl said: Your soul has become confused. If this were truly Lilith whom you had seen in your dreams, then the amulets would have driven her away. A *tzaddik* of your spiritual power has nothing to fear from the demons who prey upon men's lusts.

But now you will ask me: If this was not Lilith, then who else could it have been? I will tell you: It was the *Shekhinah*, the feminine consort of the Throne of Glory, the Divine Presence Herself. She is calling out to you. She seeks your embrace in order to heal a rupture that must be repaired. Your prayers and spells cannot drive her away, because she is an aspect of the Holy One Himself in His Infinite Splendor and Glory—an aspect of the very divine power that you draw down with your amulets.

Noach, however, protested in reply: This cannot be the *Shekhinah*—it is a terrible sin even to think such a thought. The *Shekhinah* is a Chaste and Righteous Queen Who has wandered in sorrowful exile alongside Her children Israel. She weeps for our sufferings and waits patiently for the Messiah to come, may it be speedily and in our days. Yet the woman in my dreams acted like a whore to arouse my lusts.

Berl sighed and said: She is no whore, but you saw her that way because your sinful soul is confused—your lusts were aroused by the Polish lady, and now all women appear like her in your dreams. But she is not trying to lure you into sin. She needs to unite with you in order to elevate the sparks of divine light trapped in this lowly world. Yet you mistook the husk—the rind—for the sweet nourishing fruit within.

Listen to me: I will make arrangements to take you away from here, so that you can see clearly again the difference between the holy and the sinful. And we will pray for the *Shekhinah* to come to you so that you can complete the sacred task in which she seeks your help.

IX. The Pilgrimage of the Tzaddik

NOACH COULD NOT believe his ears: The idea that the *Shekhinah*, the Divine Presence Herself, would appear to him as an immodest woman trying to lure him into disgusting sins was so absurd that he wondered if Berl had gone mad. And so, he avoided any further discussions with his good friend about the torments of his dreams. Although those torments continued to afflict him each night.

Several weeks after their strange conversation, Berl came to Noach late one night, after evening prayers, and said: We must go now. The carriage is ready. You shall embrace the *Shekhinah* tonight and achieve the unification and elevation of the holy sparks trapped in this lowly world. These great *mitzvot* will rid you of your wretched dreams.

At first, Noach refused to go. But then Berl asked what he had to be worried about—it was not as if Berl, perish the thought, was going to place Noach in any danger. Either Berl would free Noach from his nightmares once and for all or else Noach would just be where he was now, battling the apparitions that would not leave him be.

Noach reflected: Berl had always acted with kindness and generosity, and given him sage counsel. The Throne of Glory Itself had ordered Berl to descend to this world to be a staff upon which he could lean. And as to Berl's bizarre words about the *Shekhinah*? Well, maybe the wisdom of an angel was beyond the finite, limited understanding of a mortal man.

And so, Noach agreed to go with Berl.

As soon as they were both seated in the carriage, the horses sped out of the town and into the winding forest roads. Since the high tree branches blocked the moon and the stars, Noach could see nothing around him but darkness. He shuddered in terror.

Berl placed his hand on Noach's knee and said: Even though you may pass through the valley of the shadow of death, you shall fear no evil, for *HaShem* is with you and His rod and His staff shall comfort and protect you. You are being put to a great test. The Holy One, Blessed be He, has given you fame and wealth and tremendous spiritual power. But you have grown complacent and your faith is ebbing—the angels of the Heavenly Court can see these things written clearly on your forehead. You must now undertake the new task set before you: To go from healing Jews of their earthly afflictions to healing the *Shekhinah* of the pain of Her spiritual exile.

The way forward may be dark, as you can see. Drink this brandy, it will ease your nerves.

Noach felt Berl hand him a small flask. After fumbling a bit in the blackness, Noach managed to unscrew the top and pour its contents down his dry throat. As the liquid spread through his limbs, he felt himself grow so numb as to almost dissolve into the night around him. He felt not so much asleep—for he did not dream and he did not rest—as temporarily dead, as if his body had lost its spark of life and his soul was waiting patiently to be scooped out of his inert flesh by the Angel of Death.

When Noach emerged again into full consciousness, he was lying naked on a bed in a windowless room lit only by a small, red-glowing lamp. There seemed to be a light, transparent mist in the air that made everything around him appear blurred.

Then the mist parted and he beheld a tall, beautiful woman in a white robe that resembled a *kittel*. Her golden hair fell to her waist, and her sensuous lips smiled at him. She knelt down beside Noach and pinched his nose tightly, forcing his mouth to open. And into his mouth she poured a purplish liquid.

The drink tasted sweet but cold upon Noach's tongue. He felt that his senses had been suddenly heightened—he could hear every slight noise, smell every faint scent, and each touch sent tremors vibrating and humming throughout his body.

Yet at the same time he felt as helpless and adrift as if he were caught in a dream.

The woman slipped off her robe, lay down next to him, and stroked his cheek. Then they embraced. Noach felt such exquisite pleasure—an intensity he could not have imagined possible—but his thoughts were hazy and would not focus or cohere. Eventually, the pleasure faded away and he fell asleep.

When he awoke, Noach was lying naked in the same room, by the same red light, and the same woman greeted him again in her white robe. Once more, she poured the elixir down his throat, before embracing him and giving her favors. And even though this cycle repeated itself many times, Noach never spoke to the woman nor did she speak to him. He felt, vaguely, that their souls were uniting to perform some great spiritual task, but his thoughts were unable to penetrate any further. In his intervals of sleep, he had no more dreams of demon women, or of anything else; he collapsed into a heavy, slowly breathing, barely alive blackness.

But then the reverie ended. When Noach awoke this last time, the beautiful woman with the elixirs was nowhere to be seen. The red light was also gone, and in its place was a harsh candle shining right into his eyes. A hoarse, female voice shouted at him in Polish: Up, you filthy, stinking *zhyd*. Your money is spent. Get out! I am not running a poorhouse for Jew beggars.

Noach wiped the haze of sleep from his eyes and started, slowly and stiffly, to sit up. Then he felt a bony, calloused hand grab his arm and force him to his feet. Coming to his senses, he found himself standing naked before an angry, wrinkled old Polish peasant woman in a greasy kerchief.

He asked her, in his halting Polish, where he was and how he had gotten there.

She yelled back at him: Either you give me more money or you get out.

Noach asked: Where are my clothes? I will leave, but I need my clothes.

She snapped back: I don't know where you put your clothes but you can't stay if you don't pay. Fine, I will get you some clothes and then you will go.

The woman left the room and returned a couple of minutes later with a dirty, wrinkled outfit that a Polish serf would wear in the fields. Having no other choice, Noach put it on. The woman then led him out through a long hallway flanked by many similar bedrooms on either side. Noach could hear soft moaning sounds leaking out from underneath the closed doors.

At the end of the hallway, they reached a large wooden door. The woman violently yanked it open and shoved Noach outside. He stumbled down several steps into a street in a town he did not recognize. The sun was shining so brutally that he was forced to bend over and shield his eyes. He then felt a sudden nausea, and vomited a heap of semi-solid purplish liquids onto the ground.

He looked around for either Berl or the coachman but neither was anywhere to be seen.

While he was vomiting in the street, a crowd of Poles and Jews gathered around, pointing at him and laughing. From their comments, he gathered that he had been in a brothel. Filled with shame and disgust with himself, Noach burst into tears. He wished to grab a knife and scrape off his skin. But with nothing else at hand, he settled for beating himself with his fists.

After a while, the crowd dispersed. Noach wandered along the road leading out of the town, not entirely sure where he was going. Eventually, he met a Jewish beggar, who gave him directions back to his own town. Noach was relieved to learn that he had not traveled far; he would reach home by evening.

X. The Descent of the Tzaddik

THE WAY BACK turned out to be a little longer than Noach
had thought, and he did not reach his *shtetl* until after midnight. But
he did not mind the late hour—at least no one was awake to see him
in those ridiculous *goyische* peasant clothes. He knocked softly on the
front door to Berl's house, and a servant let him in. Noach darted
up to his bedroom, tore off his clothes, and lay down beneath his
familiar thick blanket.

The next morning he took stock of what had happened—how
Berl had seemingly drugged and abandoned him, without even the
shirt on his back, in a filthy brothel. And in that brothel, in his
delirium, he had sinned over and over again with some *shikse* whore.

He had to repent. He would send away all the pilgrims and the
rich men. He would spend his days in fasting and prayer.

There was also the matter of Berl. How could Berl have tricked
him so cruelly and left him in such a shameful place? Unless perhaps
something had happened to Berl? He could have been robbed or
worse in that dark forest. Something or someone must have
prevented Berl from coming to his aid—he was sure of it.

After dressing and washing, Noach went downstairs. The
house, though, was deathly quiet—a quiet that weighed heavily on

his shoulders. When he reached the kitchen, Noach spied a servant and asked her: Where are all my guests, all the pilgrims?

She replied: Gone. And new ones have stopped coming.

And the disciples, he asked, where are they?

They are together in the woods. They said they will return after they have discussed whatever it is they need to discuss.

And Berl? Where is Berl?

The servant sighed deeply. She said that Reb Berl had not been seen since he had left with Reb Noach in the big carriage in the middle of the night a few days ago.

Noach decided to go to the synagogue for his morning prayers, as he no longer had a *minyan* in his home to pray with. And perhaps one of the householders there could give him a clue as to Berl's whereabouts.

But when he approached the synagogue courtyard, the *shammes* barred his way. Reb Noach, the *shammes* said, you are no longer permitted to cross this threshold. The *parnasim* of this town have issued a ban, a *cherem*, against you. You may not pray with this holy community and no righteous Jew may have any dealings with you.

Noach asked why he had been placed under the ban. He swore that he must have been the victim of some unfounded, vicious slander.

The *shammes* replied: Slander? Do you know how many Jews with their own eyes saw you walk out of the brothel in the town of Y? Or witnessed your disgusting behavior through a window— because you and your *shikse* lacked the decency even to close the blinds! You are a fraud—you pretended to be a holy *tzaddik*, a saint, but your eyes lust for filthy *shikse* whores. Be gone! Leave us!

Noach was taken aback. How had the Jews in his town already learned of his shame? He had assumed –or hoped—that they would not know—or at least, they would not know *yet*. But the *shammes* clearly knew. And as the *shammes* was not particularly clever or curious, he could only know if he had been told by many others.

But then again, he had been publicly humiliated after being thrown out of a brothel. And with so many pilgrims passing through his court, there were many Jews who would recognize his face and know his name.

Noach was tempted, for a brief moment, to try to explain that he had been tricked and drugged, but what would have been the point? He had been seen leaving the brothel—he could not deny he had been there. And if he had been there, he had sinned and now he must repent.

Still, he had one more question for the *shammes*: Have you seen Reb Berl?

The *shammes* did not reply, but instead shook his head and walked back inside the synagogue.

Noach returned to Berl's house and sat down alone in the room where he had formerly received long lines of pilgrims. The shame now ran hot and quick through Noach's body. He wept, and banged his head against the stone floor until his forehead gushed with blood. Noach vowed to repent. He would fast for the four days before the next *Shabbat*. He would spend his every waking hour begging the Holy One, Blessed be He, for forgiveness. He would put aside his learned, scholarly books and instead recite Psalms, like an ignorant village Jew who could barely read a single Hebrew letter in his *siddur*.

And so, for the next two days and nights, Noach fasted, recited Psalms, and begged *HaShem* to forgive his sins. He rebuked himself harshly: Not only for lusting after a Gentile prostitute, but also for his overweening pride and arrogance. He had reveled in empty flattery and neglected his studies of the Torah and the *Kabbalah*. He had lost the humility of a true *tzaddik*, who never forgets that he is but dust born from a putrid drop.

But on the morning of the third day, his penance was interrupted. Into the room where he was praying burst a dozen of his disciples, with their wives and children in tow. When they beheld Noach, they erupted in shouts of joy and cries of hallelujah, and they embraced him warmly.

Noach was bewildered, for his disciples must have heard of his great shame and humiliation. So how could they be rejoicing in his presence? Had they all gone mad? Or was this a test? Had the Holy One, Blessed be He, decided to allow Ashmedai, King of the Demons, to test the genuineness of his atonement by sending the illusion of loyal, worshipful followers back to him, to see if he had truly overcome his pride and arrogance?

With these thoughts swirling about his mind, Noach said to them: How can you show me such honor? I am the lowest of the low, the foulest hypocrite and the most disgusting sinner. I have spent days and nights drinking and fornicating with a *shikse* whore. I am guilty. I am filthy. For my many and terrible sins, the elders of this holy community have rightly put me under the ban. I must fast and atone. I will leave this place soon enough. You, too, must leave me. Show me the dishonor and contempt that I merit for my wretched deeds. Insult me, mock me—I must be punished for my crimes.

But the crowd of disciples did not back away, nor did they offer any rebuke. Instead, one of their number, a pale, skinny man named Mendel, stepped forward and answered Noach: Holy *tzaddik*, master and teacher, we know all about your so-called sins. At first there were only vague rumors that you had departed secretly, in the dead of night, in order to satisfy some degraded, base lust. Then word reached us, and everyone else in this town, that you had been seen exiting a brothel in clothes that were obviously not your own. The pilgrims fled; the rich men pretended they had never sought your counsel; and, as you said, the householders and rabbi issued a *cherem* and put you under the ban.

We were unsure which path to follow. Each of us had left the town where he had dwelt in order to sit at your feet and hear your wisdom and spread your Torah. We had sold businesses and

abandoned trades to devote ourselves without distraction to your
holy work. And we had insisted that our wives and children follow
us. Were we deluded fools who had squandered everything to kiss
the feet of a fraud? What would we say to the Jews back in our
former towns—that we had left them to bask in the shame of a
wretched sinner?

But this couldn't be the truth of these matters—for we had
seen, in you, something holy and beautiful, a shimmering spark of
divine light. We had witnessed your healing powers. We knew there
must be a great mystery hidden beneath your strange conduct that
we, with our limited understanding, could not grasp.

And then we—that is, all of us whom you see assembled
together now—dreamt the same dream in the same night: That your
companion, Reb Berl, told us to journey to a remote hut in the
forest, where he would reveal the secret truths hidden beneath your
actions.

We knew it could not be an accident that we had all dreamed
the same dream at the same time. So we went to that hut in the forest
and prayed for guidance.

At dusk, Reb Berl entered the hut. At first, we could barely see
him in the spreading darkness. But then his face lit up with a glorious
radiance, as if there was a bright lamp shining from within his
forehead. By this light we could see him as clearly as if it were the
middle of the day.

Berl spoke to us and revealed the truth of your secret, holy
mission. This is what he said: I know your faith is wavering. Even
though you have many times witnessed the saintliness and spiritual
power of our master and teacher, the holy *tzaddik* Noach, you have
now learned that he has spent the past few days in the embraces of
a *shikse* whore. You believe that our Noach must either be a
righteous saint or a filthy sinner. He cannot be both, and yet you
have seen him be both. And so, you are perplexed.

To what can this be compared? There once was a king who had a beloved daughter. One day, her father sent her away from the castle, for she had much to learn about the world beyond its gates. She wandered far and wide until she came to a village with fine weather and lovely apple trees. There, she chose to rest for a while. At first, she remembered that she was a princess and held herself aloof from the villagers. But the longer she stayed, and the friendlier she became with them, the more she grew accustomed to the ways of the coarse villagers. Little by little she abandoned her royal customs until eventually she acted and spoke just like any other village woman.

After a time, her father the king missed the company of his daughter and wished to bring her back to his castle. And so, he dispatched three noblemen from his court to find her and escort her home. The three noblemen discovered that the princess had settled in that village. The first nobleman stood at the village gates in all his finery and demanded that the princess come out and join him, so that he could return her to her father the king. But the princess, egged on by the village women, laughed at him and told him to go away.

The second nobleman tried a different approach. Still wearing his finery, he rode his horse into the village square and right up to the princess. He rebuked her for her coarse dress and poor manners. He reminded her of her royal blood and demanded that she mount his horse behind him so they could return at once to her father the king. But the princess had drifted so far from her royal upbringing that she spat in the second nobleman's face and drove him out with angry curses.

The third nobleman, however, used a different tack. He discarded his expensive clothing and mighty horse, and instead donned the dirty rags of a simple villager. When he approached the princess, he did not upbraid her for acting like a peasant. To the contrary, he pretended to be just as vulgar as she was and so gained her trust and friendship. Slowly, over time, he was able to persuade her that she was actually a princess. She eventually agreed to return with him to her father the king.

The meaning of the parable is this: Once the princess had lingered too long in exile from the king, she had forgotten that she had ever been a princess at all. To raise her back up to her proper station, the third nobleman had to descend to her level and pretend to be a coarse villager. Only then was he able to win her confidence and slowly lead her back to her father the king. In other words, in order to raise her up, the nobleman first had to descend into the far depths in which she had fallen.

Our master and teacher, the holy *tzaddik* Noach, is that third nobleman. His King—Who is the One True and Only King of Kings, the Holy One, Blessed be He—called to him to go out and find His lost princess and return her from her exile to the Throne of Glory.

But the princess whom Noach must redeem is not one, but many. When a Jewish soul is stained with sin, the Heavenly Court will send it back down to this lowly world in a new incarnation to repair itself and atone for its many sins. Yet such souls often forget that they are exalted and holy. Noach is seeking out these fallen souls—to go down to their degraded level and then raise them back up to the level of sanctity.

That *shikse* prostitute was just such a soul. In a prior incarnation, she had been a Jewish wife and mother married to a mighty Torah scholar. But her *yetzer ha-ra*, her evil inclination, led her astray, and she sinned repeatedly with a *goy* who labored in the nobleman's stables, an ignoramus who could not even read his own language, much less the holy tongue. Her adultery tormented the heart of her pure, scholarly husband throughout the length of his days.

When her soul was sent back down to this world, she was reborn as the child of Gentile servants in the household of a wealthy, pious, and learned Jewish merchant. Yet instead of being drawn to the atmosphere of holiness and Torah in that house, once again her lusts overpowered her and she wound up in a brothel.

When Noach came to her, he beheld a soul attired in a shimmering white *kittel*. He reached down to her and pulled her back up. You may ask why he touched her if he was not acting out of lust. However, you know the reason: Noach heals wounds and cures illnesses by the touch of his hand as he recites his blessing—you have seen this wonder many times. Many of *you* have been healed by his touch. Would you deny the same blessing to her?

This is a terrible burden that Noach has taken upon himself. By descending to the level where the princess wallows in filth, he appears to common fools, like this town's Jews, to be just as wretched as her. Indeed, the first two noblemen in my parable are like the rabbis of our age: They will not descend to the level of the sinner in exile from the king. No, they look down upon her from their lofty heights, brimming with arrogance and contempt, and command her to raise herself up to their level. And while they do not soil their precious garments or risk a word of rebuke, they have also done nothing to redeem the masses of fallen souls who swarm about them.

Now that you, the most steadfast disciples of our master and teacher, the light of our exile, the holy *tzaddik* Reb Noach, know the truth of these wondrous matters, you must firm up his faith and keep him to the path of righteousness. For Noach too is wavering and doubting. His heart is pained at the loss of the honor and esteem that he once enjoyed. He will be tempted to repent and become just like the first two noblemen who never discarded their noble finery. Yet remember they could not save the princess. There are many souls suffering in exile from their king whom Noach can redeem— must redeem—if only he will have the courage to descend into the world of sin and filth and then lift them back up.

Those were the last words that Reb Berl spoke to us. For suddenly, the radiant glow from within his forehead turned a fiery red—like the sun at twilight—and steam burst forth from his ears and nostrils. His limbs trembled and there was a great noise, like a thunder clap, and in an instant, he had vanished. We knew then, without a doubt, that Berl was an angel sent down to our lowly world to guide us in the path of righteousness and Torah.

And so, master and teacher, holy *tzaddik*, we have returned to you. Unlike the fools who rebuke you, we understand the esoteric truths concealed beneath your strange actions. We will help you find more souls mired in the depths whom your touch can heal.

Noach, however, was appalled at what he had just heard, and he sternly reproved his disciples: How can you say my conduct was holy? I am soiled, disgusting, vile—I must atone. Leave me and find another master, a better teacher, one who can guide you in the ways of the Torah. I shall soon take up a wanderer's staff and live as a beggar, going barefoot from town to town. I will devote my every breath to pleading with *HaShem* to forgive me.

To Noach's surprise, his words did not seem to shame or even anger his disciples. Instead, they exchanged concerned, compassionate looks with each other, as if they were figuring out how best to help a man screaming in delirium from a raging fever.

The disciple Mendel stepped forward once more. He calmly explained that, after the disciples had returned to the house, they had searched Berl's room for books or manuscripts that could help guide them. Although they had found no such writings, they did come across several crates filled with liquor. Perhaps the holy *tzaddik* should have a taste, to calm his nerves?

Mendel reached into his pocket and pulled out a flask. Remembering how Berl had drugged him, Noach recoiled in terror and screamed at his disciples to leave him alone. But rather than heed his words, two disciples grabbed Noach's arms and then Mendel pinched his nose and poured the liquor down his throat.

As Noach felt his body grow numb and his consciousness fade away, he heard Mendel speaking to him, as if from across a vast distance in a faint, hollow voice: Master and teacher, holy *tzaddik*, please forgive us. We wish to obey your words. However, your spirit has been confused and deceived by the hordes of the *sitra achra*, the demonic realm, who fear your holy work. Once your mind is unclouded, you will thank us, with tears in your eyes, for not being fooled by the false words dribbling off of your tongue at this moment—words that a demon in your throat is uttering in your righteous name. Rest now, master and teacher, and when you awake, we will be there by your side—we, your true disciples, we who understand.

Noach wanted to cry out that it was Mendel who had gone mad and been tricked by demons—that the Holy One, Blessed be He, would never sanction sins as awful as Noach's sins with the *shikse* whore—but he had lost the strength to move his lips. With his limbs growing heavier, Noach soon could not keep his eyelids open any longer and he drifted off into a black, dreamless abyss.

XI. The Metamorphosis of the Tzaddik

WHEN NOACH AWOKE, he was lying in his bed. Yet when he tried to sit up, he found that his arms and legs had been tied to the bedposts. After calling out for help, the disciple Mendel came into his room and said: Master and teacher, holy *tzaddik*, please forgive us. Until we can be sure that your soul has been freed from evil and temptation, we cannot let you move about. If you were to run away and abandon your sacred mission—abandon all those souls whom you could save—no, we could not permit that to happen.

But here, I have food and drink for you.

Mendel quickly recited the blessings over this meal and then brought tea with sugar to Noach's lips, which he greedily drank down—for the warm liquid soothed his parched throat. Then Mendel fed him pieces of bread spread with plum jam.

Once Noach finished eating, Mendel quietly left the room. Alone again, Noach closed his eyes and prayed to be delivered from his captivity. He promised *HaShem* that, if his prayers were answered, he would devote his remaining days to atonement for his many sins.

An hour or so later, Mendel returned, with the other disciples in tow. They were wearing white robes and held prayer books in their hands. Mendel led a woman to Noach's bedside. She, too, was wearing a *kittel*. She was plump, with unwashed yellow hair and a face furrowed by her first creeping wrinkles.

Mendel explained that this woman was another Gentile prostitute. They had paid extra for permission to temporarily remove her from the brothel where she usually plied her trade. As Noach had already once before redeemed a fallen soul trapped in a whore's body, Mendel felt certain that he could perform the same miracle again. After all, the *tzaddik* must descend to the lowest level in order to grasp and uplift the sparks of holiness trapped in the mire and the bog.

Mendel then removed a flask from his pocket and sprinkled a few drops of Berl's elixir upon Noach's lips. Despite his best efforts to spit it out, the liquor slid rapidly down his throat. As he felt the liquid move through his body, the woman standing indifferently and bored above him suddenly began to glow, as if a holy light, a divine spark, were trapped within her sinful flesh. Noach reached out for this light, but his hands were too tightly bound to the bedposts.

Mendel instructed the woman to lie on top of Noach. In response, she undressed mechanically and apathetically mounted him. Mendel and the other disciples surrounded his bed in a semicircle, opened their prayer books, and began to chant Psalms. Noach told himself that he should be appalled and disgusted, but his head felt light from the powerful liquor and his thoughts could not cohere. And he still beheld the light shining forth from inside the *shikse* whore.

After his body had tasted its pleasure, Noach collapsed into a stupor. When he awoke, he was alone again. From the dark window, he could tell that it was nighttime. In a moment of sudden clarity, he realized he had sinned once more with a prostitute and burst into violent sobs. He was disgusting, he was filthy, he had abandoned the Torah and given into his evil inclination. The liquor had blinded him with the illusion of a holy light. But it was only an illusion: There was no divine spark inside that sinning whore, just a putrid, rotting soul waiting its turn to receive just punishment in the next world.

Noach cried out to the Holy One, Blessed be He, and begged to be released from this torment. *He* wished only to repent—it was Mendel and the other disciples who insisted that he must sin—who forced him to sin. If only his bonds could be loosened, he could escape and walk the path of righteousness.

After a while, he fell back asleep, until he was woken again by Mendel and the other disciples. The sun was now shining harshly, and hurt his eyes.

Mendel praised Noach for making another holy descent into the realm of sin in order to raise up the divine light concealed and trapped inside the *shikse* prostitute.

In reply, Noach exploded with rage: How can you call me master and teacher yet force me into such shame? I was already a worthless pig rolling in mud and excrement, and yet you are compelling me to pile even more sins onto my already blackened soul. Please, I beg you, free me so that I may go forth to wander and repent. Perhaps I may be able to merit earning back some meager portion in the World to Come.

Mendel, though, sighed and shook his head. And then he said: Do you remember how I first came to you, holy *tzaddik*? My wife, my beautiful Feige, had a terrible cough. She could not stop coughing, day and night, and she could not sleep. Soon she was coughing up her blood, and not just drops, but whole fistfuls. The doctors said it was hopeless. But then I brought her here, to you. You, master and teacher, put your hand on her cheek and recited the loveliest blessing—your voice was like a nightingale singing.

And when you were done, my Feige stood up and was completely cured—it was a miracle—an actual miracle, in our days, like Elisha reviving the dead son of the Shunamite woman. I knew at that moment that you were the greatest saint and sage of our generation. I sold my shop and abandoned my livelihood and moved my family here, so we could serve you and walk in your ways. My father and my brothers told me I was a mad fool and they swore they would never send me a single *złoty*, no matter how desperate a beggar I became. But I paid them no heed, for I trusted in the Holy One, Blessed be He. And *HaShem* provided for us as your court prospered.

But then the fickle pilgrims, who had once pleaded for your blessing, deserted you. They said your crossing the threshold of a brothel proved you were a hypocrite and a fraud. I was tempted to agree—for how can a great *tzaddik* commit such an abominable sin? I feared my father had been right to ridicule me as a fool.

Yet if you were a fraud, then how had you performed so many miracles? Once or twice, and I could see how that could be a clever trick. But to heal as many as you healed, that kind of power can only come from the Holy One, Blessed be He, in all His Glory. When Berl revealed your sacred task—how you must heal and elevate the most wretchedly fallen souls by first sinking to their degraded level—I realized that you were the greatest *tzaddik* who had ever lived. For it is easy to be like the noblemen in Berl's parable who never shed their noble finery—these are the rabbis of our generation who will never go near sin, and who will keep the raiment of their souls impeccably spotless. *They* would never dare to reach into the depths to rescue souls trapped in the mire. *They* would rather let such souls wither and rot and suffer. But not you, master and teacher.

Yesterday, when you lay with the whore, your eyes were aflame with a holy light—your eyes burst with yearning for your Creator and His Holy Torah. There was no trace of lust or evil in your radiant face. Can you not see how holy this work is that you must do? No one else will repair these fallen souls, because no other *tzaddik* will take upon himself the shame of descending to their wretched level. You are their only hope for redemption—how can you abandon them to wallow in your own selfish guilt?

Noach was taken aback. Mendel was right, of course—no rabbi or scholar would soil his honor by mixing with the most loathsome sinners. Or, if he were to be redeemed, then the sinner must take the first step and choose the path of atonement. But what about the sinners so lost in their sins that they could not find their way out— like the princess in the parable who could no longer recall her royal birth and considered herself to be just another coarse village woman? Was there a spark of holiness left in them to redeem, if only a true *tzaddik* would condescend to look? Both times when he had sinned with prostitutes, Noach had beheld a light so brilliant that it could not have been an earthly vision. Maybe *HaShem* was guiding him to these souls in need of healing?

And so, Noach told Mendel and the other disciples that he agreed with them and would willingly descend to the level of the greatest sinners so that he could raise up and redeem the holy sparks of light hidden within their souls.

In fact, he ordered his disciples to invite the worst sinners in the town for *Shabbat* dinner the next evening. In order to fully descend to their putrid level, Noach insisted that the dinner be *treyf* —roasted pork with cheese—and the guests would light their pipes to further desecrate *Shabbat*.

His disciples rejoiced at these words and freed him from his bonds. They prepared a Sabbath feast exactly as he had requested, full of *treyf* foods and *treyf* wine and sinful Jews. Noach spent the entire holiday with these sinners, descending to their level: Drinking to excess, eating pork, gambling at cards, and neglecting his prayers and studies. He felt ill at ease—with each sin he felt a dagger thrust of silent shame into his heart—and he longed to peak, if only for a brief moment, at the weekly Torah portion. But he forced himself to hold firm: He must fall to their level and convince them that he could be trusted, that he was a sinner like them.

At one point, on Saturday afternoon, so sick with shame that he could bear it no longer, Noach left Berl's house and vomited in the street. When he was finished, he looked up at the faces of a few pious Jews passing by. Their eyes burned with disgust. But then he remembered: The pious souls passing him in the street did not need his aid; it was the wayward souls inside his house who were in desperate need of healing.

In the week that followed, his *Shabbat* guests returned often and brought their Polish and Ukrainian friends, both men and women, with them. The house quickly became a den of gambling and drink. The women who came freely sold their favors in the first bed or couch or nook that they found. At Mendel's urging, Noach paid to take each of these *shikse* women to bed.

Yet no matter how far he descended into the world of sin, Noach could no longer see visions of holy light from within these sinful souls. He tried drinking the liquor in Berl's flasks, but the liquor did not help; it only dulled his reason and inflamed his lusts. He could feel the wisdom of the Torah dwindle and fade in his memory, as if the teachings of the holy sages were fleeing from him in their shame.

One night, he abstained from drink. With his reason now clear, he watched in despair as two miserable criminals, a Jew and a Pole who stole horses together, got drunk and fought with knives over who was entitled to what share of their illicit profits. The blood from their wounds splashed all over the tablecloths and floor and walls, staining everything.

Unable to bear this disgrace, Noach went outside. It was late at night, and quite dark. Wandering alone beneath a weak sliver of a yellow moon, he heard the sound of weeping. Approaching closer, he came upon a young woman standing on a porch and shouting out to Heaven to save her little son from death—he had been running a terrible fever, the doctor said it was hopeless, but how could her Creator be so cruel as to snatch away such a beautiful child, barely a year old, from his mother who loved him so much? What terrible sin had she committed to merit such an awful punishment? She begged the Holy One, Blessed be He, for just a few more years so she could see him grow and kiss his cheek and hear him call her mama.

His heart moved by this prayer, Noach ran to her, told her that he would heal her child, and then burst into her home. The grieving mother ran in after him, screaming that she knew exactly who and what he was—he was that filthy fraud and hypocrite, the so-called *tzaddik* who slept with *shikse* whores.

I am no fraud, Noach replied. I have healed hundreds, thousands, of Jews, many of them children. Let me bless your son and the boy will be healed.

Noach tried to recite a blessing, but he could no longer recall the Hebrew words he had so often used to heal the sick. Wracking his brain, desperate to save this dying child, he spat out whatever Hebrew phrases he could quickly dredge up from his fogged memory, all of which together sounded like a blessing—or so he hoped. Then he placed his hands on the baby's tiny, soft cheeks, which burned with fever.

At his touch, the baby screamed even louder and his skin turned a hideous, putrid green. And then the child stopped crying. Noach felt relieved at first, thinking he had healed the boy. But he soon noticed that the child had stopped moving and his little chest no longer rose and fell with the rhythm of breathing.

The boy's mother rushed over and put a feather under his nose. When she saw there was no breath, she let out a tremendous wail of grief and accused Noach of murder.

In terror and shame, Noach ran away, back into the dark night.

XII. The Final Revelation

AFTER NOACH HAD returned to his home, he sat down in a corner and tried to soothe his guilt, reflecting that The Holy One, Blessed be He, alone decides who shall live and who shall die. He, Noach, never had the power to annul the decrees of the Heavenly Court. At most, he had been an instrument through which *HaShem* had chosen to heal those whom He had already decided to spare. Thus, it must have been decreed in the higher worlds that this child would die.

Still, he felt the child's death was also a message to him: That he must repent. He had been mad to think that he could achieve holiness through sin—the only thing sin begets is more and worse sin. As he no longer knew where his holy books were—even assuming that they had not all been used as kindling by the miserable company that had entrenched itself in his house—Noach locked himself in his bedroom and tried as hard as he could to remember his prayers. Yet the Hebrew words fled from his lips. He was now lower than the most ignorant beggar, who at least knew a Psalm or two.

In his desperation, Noach concentrated his thoughts on the forms of the Hebrew letters. He implored the Throne of Glory to accept this pitiful offering of the Hebrew alphabet and use the letters to form the prayers that he, with his many and horrible sins, had forgotten. Noach continued repeating his simple prayer until sleep overcame him. As he faded into the black oblivion of rest, he promised himself that, when he awoke, he would leave this place and take up his staff to wander as a beggar and a penitent across the holy communities of Poland and Lithuania. He would learn again how to pray and he would study the humblest, most heartfelt *musar* teachings of the holy sages of blessed memory.

But when Noach awoke the next morning, he could not rise from his bed because of a sharp, burning pain in his manly parts. When he lifted the blanket to look down upon his flesh, he beheld, to his horror, that his manly parts had turned a gangrenous green and yellow and were dotted with pustules oozing thick, white puss. At the sight of his own rotting, diseased flesh, Noach felt suddenly nauseous and vomited over the side of his bed.

He screamed out in agony and begged for help. Mendel and the other disciples broke the lock on his door and immediately sent for the doctor and the apothecary. But both men refused to come— Noach and his house were so disreputable that they did not wish to stain their honor by being associated with them in any way.

So, with no other choice, Mendel and the other disciples did their best to nurse Noach back to health. Yet their efforts were unavailing, and the disease continued to spread. Noach could keep no food down, and barely any water, and his forehead burned with a raging fever.

And then he awoke one morning, all alone, with the sun shining brightly into his room. The house was strangely quiet, as if all the gamblers and drunkards had departed. Nor did he hear the whispers or shuffles of his disciples. At the same time, the pain and the fever were gone. He gingerly sat up and let out a gentle yawn.

Suddenly, at the foot of the bed, he saw Berl, standing tall and resplendent in a white *kittel*. Noach called out to him with tears of joy and said how much he had missed his old friend's love and wisdom.

Speaking no words in reply, Berl raised his hand in the air and made a circular motion with his index finger. Now Noach found himself back in the ruined hut in the forest where, so long ago, he had used secret kabbalistic formulae to make an ascent of his soul into the higher worlds—the ascent that had started him down this path that had ended in such sin and shame.

Berl said to Noach: Your task is complete.

And with those words, Berl tore Noach's soul out from his body and then the emptied-out flesh burst into flames.

Other Books by Barak Bassman

About the Author

Barak A. Bassman received a B.A. in Classics from Grinnell College and a law degree from the New York University School of Law. He practices law in Philadelphia, Pennsylvania, and lives in the Philadelphia suburbs with his wife and two children. He is the author of, among other works, *Repentance: A Tale of Demons in Old Jewish Poland, King Solomon and Ashmedai: A Wisdom Tale, Necromancy of the Demon Maiden: A Gothic Tale of Podolia, The Vampire and the Wandering Jew, The Emissary from Mezeritch: A Dark Hasidic Tale, The Holy Sinner: A Gothic Tale of the Baal Shem Tov, The Baal Shem Tov and the Heretic: A Sabbatean Tale, The Starvation Dybbuk: A Cruel Tale of Love and Exorcism,* and *The Twisted Path of the Hidden Saint: An Occult Tale of the Baal Shem Tov,* and *The Mad Disciples of Jacob Frank: A Tale of the Demon Goddess.*

www.ingramcontent.com/pod-product-compliance
Lightning Source LLC
Chambersburg PA
CBHW030510130626
46549CB00007B/2919